A COMPREH
FRAMEWORK FOR
TEACHING DIGITAL
CITIZENSHIP IN SCHOOLS

FUTURE PROOF

TOM HARRISON, GIANFRANCO POLIZZI,
SOPHIE MURFIN, LEE PEACHEY

JOHN CATT

First published 2022

by John Catt Educational Ltd,
15 Riduna Park, Station Road,
Melton, Woodbridge IP12 1QT

Tel: +44 (0) 1394 389850
Email: enquiries@johncatt.com
Website: www.johncatt.com

ISBN: 978 1 915261 12 0

Set and designed by John Catt Educational Limited

REVIEWS

Futureproof is a unique book and one that is timely given the current education climate and development in digital technology. The authors provide a clear framework for school leaders and teachers to develop a shared language. Highly recommended.

Michael Chiles, author of *The CRAFT of Assessment* and *The Feedback Pendulum*

Much has been said about digital citizenship, but do we really know what it is and why it matters? This clear-sighted volume sets out an exciting and practical approach for teachers that will inspire students to explore their agency, ambition and responsibility in a digital world.

Sonia Livingstone, director, Digital Futures Commission; professor of social psychology, London School of Economics and Political Science

Futureproof is ahead of the curve. At present, there is no real framework nor book out there that encourages educators in all phases to seriously consider how we teach our pupils about digital citizenship. Given the ever-changing landscape, arguably accelerated by the rise of new technological platforms during the pandemic, this book is ever more relevant, needed and on the money. It is a fantastic read and an education in itself. Bravo!

Sam Strickland, principal, the Duston School, Northampton; author of *Education Exposed* and *Education Exposed 2*

We all have a responsibility to support young people with knowledge of digital citizenship. More than ever, schools and children need a framework and support to help them navigate ever-changing digital technologies. This is a brilliant hands-on, practical guide and a must-read for any leader or teacher.

Michael Hamilton OBE, founder, Commando Joe's

A perfect synthesis of what matters, what works and what to do next to equip students for success in the complexity of digital evolution. *Futureproof* offers a framework for adaptation by schools, giving a foundation to face an ever-changing world though values, experiences and management of risk. It offers expertise based on credible research, providing anchor points for the growth of a generation of young people who will no doubt consume content and shape our shared future more than any other in history.

Glyn Potts, headteacher, Newman RC College, Oldham

Developing our children's online character should sit central to any school improvement drive. During times that have seen an unprecedented rise in online threat, educationalists need to change mindsets.

It is a fact that the internet and 'online identity' will define our children's social, emotional and academic pathways. As educators, we must accept that teaching children only about 'online harm' will serve to push their behaviours underground and cause greater risk. We must instead equip them to identify and navigate danger and in turn create 'cyber-resilience'.

Futureproof is a refreshingly accessible evidence-based guide that feels real and current. It is fair to say that if, as leaders, we didn't perceive that digital literacy was relevant to the pupils in our school before reading this book, there remains no doubt afterwards. A must for every school leader.

Antony Bradshaw, head of school, Colmore Junior School, Birmingham

CONTENTS

PREFACE

SHOOTING IN THE DARK WHILE TRYING TO HIT A MOVING TARGET

Digital technologies are ubiquitous, so it is perhaps surprising that there is no recognised digital citizenship education framework to guide UK schools in helping pupils to live in the digital age. Digital citizenship, we believe, should be understood as the wise and responsible use of digital technologies, with a view to interacting with others and taking part in multiple domains of everyday life, from leisure and employment to civic and political life. The absence of a digital citizenship education framework gives rise to two key questions: how are pupils being taught to use digital technologies wisely, and is our current approach to digital citizenship education futureproof?

There are several reasons why there is no commonly agreed framework to guide education for digital citizenship. The primary reason is that digital technologies have evolved so rapidly over the past two decades that it has been hard for educators to keep up. Technological innovation has far outpaced curriculum innovation, meaning that we largely rely on 20th-century pedagogical approaches to prepare pupils for 21st-century life. It is therefore not surprising that, when it comes to educating for digital citizenship, many teachers feel they are shooting in the dark while trying to hit a moving target.

This is not to say that no useful advice has been published by the UK government or other civil society organisations working in the education sector. Perhaps the closest official publication to the framework we propose in this book is *Education for a Connected World*.[1] Provided by the UK Council for Internet Safety in partnership with multiple organisations, including the PSHE Association and Parent Zone, their framework offers guidance on the skills and knowledge that children should gain, through formal education, in relation to some of the key risks posed by digital technologies. More specifically, their framework focuses on eight aspects of digital education, with an emphasis on internet safety, including cyberbullying, self-identity and managing online information. These categories resonate with the key topics and learning outcomes outlined in Common Sense Education's digital citizenship curriculum.[2] Designed by the international organisation Common Sense, this curriculum is another very helpful source of advice and guidance for teachers.

The UK government has published specific advice on how to stay safe online and on aspects of digital citizenship – aspects that are included in the PSHE statutory modules of 'relationships and sex education' and 'health education'.[3] Recently, the Department for Digital, Culture, Media and Sport published an online media literacy strategy that includes a framework for what users should know in order to act as critical users of online information and to interact in meaningful and positive ways with other users.[4]

Promisingly, numerous charities, educational organisations and individuals have also developed advice and guidance linked to specific digital risks and opportunities. This guidance largely includes teaching materials and lesson plans, developed by organisations such as Childnet and Wise Kids.[5] Taken together, all this means there is plenty of inspiration for school leaders interested in making digital citizenship education more prominent in their schools. Drawing on guidance and advice when it is available, most schools educate pupils about cyberbullying, online safety, artificial intelligence, biotechnology advances and how to be a 'good' citizen online, alongside many other related topics. What we believe is lacking, however, is something more radical and less piecemeal: an approach that is proactive, not reactive. What we need is a comprehensive framework that is focused on developing knowledge, as well as the skills, competencies, values and character to help pupils flourish in the future, while also concentrating on the school policies and guidance necessary to make this possible. This is what we outline in this book: a framework for digital citizenship education that we believe is *futureproof.*

Our framework provides a coherent and comprehensive structure that echoes and complements previous frameworks and sources of advice. Crucially, it starts with schools developing their own vision for digital citizenship – one that meets the needs of the pupils they serve. The framework covers, on the one hand, the importance of implementing rules and regulations and, on the other, the development of competencies and character virtues in pupils.

We want to stress from the outset our belief that, as outlined above, there are many excellent resources available to teach digital citizenship. There are also many outstanding teachers in schools using these resources. Our contention, however, is that in many schools, digital citizenship is delivered in a somewhat ad-hoc way. This is where the Futureproof framework comes in. It will help to ensure pupils are taught about the risks and opportunities associated with digital technologies in ways that are linked to the competencies, values, character, policies and guidance that the framework promotes more cohesively. Relatedly, the framework will help to ensure that what pupils learn in science or PSHE corresponds with what they learn in assemblies or whole-school activities. It suggests that the digital citizenship education pupils receive should be built up year on year in ways that correspond to their age and maturity. Finally, the framework is designed to be flexible enough to respond to technological change and be ahead of it.

We believe Futureproof is an accessible, theory-driven, practice-based framework that can, after local adjustments, be implemented in any primary or secondary school in the UK. This book will show school leaders and teachers how they can educate for the 21st century and teach digital citizenship through a single, comprehensive, planned and coherent approach. *Futureproof* draws on all three of the most prominent moral theories (based on promoting rules, an awareness of consequences, and character virtues) to underpin a systematic approach to education for digital citizenship.

As such, *Futureproof*:

- Introduces a new digital citizenship education framework that addresses digital risks and opportunities together and holistically.

- Addresses key concerns in ways that relate to digital citizenship, including issues of online safety and security, digital literacy, online crime, employment, cyberbullying, online harms, digital wellbeing, e-learning, and civic and political participation.
- Adopts a character strengths-based approach, preparing young people for their future lives and work.
- Is not deficit-based – it celebrates the positives of digital technologies and how these can contribute to individual and societal flourishing and wellbeing.
- Aligns with current policy on online safety from the UK Department for Education and the UK Council for Internet Safety's *Education for a Connected World* framework, as well as advice from other prominent organisations including Common Sense and the NSPCC.
- Is hands-on and practical – it provides a step-by-step approach and shows, by using examples, how school leaders, teachers and others working in education can implement the framework.
- Is grounded in established theory and underpinned by research and evidence.

WHY SCHOOLS MUST ACT NOW

While policymakers in the UK have been prioritising the regulation of online platforms and the promotion of digital literacy as possible solutions to online risks, teachers, alongside parents, have a responsibility to deliver digital citizenship education. If we are to address all the risks associated with digital technologies while taking full advantage of the opportunities they offer, then tech companies, governments, parents, teachers, civil society organisations and children themselves all have a role to play. These roles are not always clear and there are often disagreements between stakeholders about who should be doing what.

The one thing we all know is that we must act now.

To explain why, an analogy with smoking might be drawn. When cigarettes were invented, the harm they caused to health was not known. We do not know, at this stage, to what extent digital technologies can not only provide considerable opportunities but also have long-term, society-wide, potentially pernicious effects on individuals' wellbeing and ability to thrive and live well collectively. It is still to be seen whether these technologies are primarily and largely beneficial or not. We need more in-depth longitudinal data before we can truly understand the impact of digital technologies such as the internet, not just on individuals' health and wellbeing but on the health and wellbeing of society more broadly. As we cannot afford to wait for this data to become available, we can and should all take action now.

Given what we currently know, policymakers and educationalists need to be proactive and pragmatic. They must develop educational approaches that minimise online harms while also (considering the freedoms and opportunities that the internet affords) providing young users with the tools, skills, knowledge and values that can enable them to thrive in the digital age.

As a result, the approach that schools adopt should have the following key features.

- **It must be pupil-centred**: it should take into account the views of pupils and real-life examples of how they experience their digital lives.
- **It should not be deterministic**: that is, it should be founded on a belief in human agency and an understanding that pupils are ultimately going to be in control of what they use digital technologies for.
- **It should be empowering**: it should encourage pupils to participate and play online and use the technologies wisely to bring benefits to themselves, others and wider society.
- **It should not be dualistic**: there should be an understanding that humans and technologies must work together in harmony. Their relationship should not be about one trumping the other.
- **It should not be indoctrinating**: that is, it should not be about 'fixing' kids or telling them how to behave online.

These are the features that define the digital citizenship education framework we introduce in this book. The common theme in all these features is that they place pupils, as autonomous rational beings, at the heart of their digital worlds. In other words, while different actors have different roles to play in order to ensure pupils are safe while using digital technologies, the outcomes of these interactions also depend on pupils themselves.

A FRAMEWORK FOUNDED ON CHARACTER

Given that pupils' decisions and actions are ultimately what will determine how they use digital technologies (and whether these are used for good and/or bad ends), the central goal of the Futureproof framework is to cultivate character and wisdom in pupils. The framework includes digital rules that schools should put in place, but it is pupils' character, values and virtues that ultimately matter. By ensuring that schools and educators establish character expectations alongside parents, pupils can be guided and supported to make wiser, responsible decisions when engaging with digital technologies. It is character, after all, that enables pupils to 'do the right thing' when no one is looking. This form of education – that is, character education – cannot be simply rules-based, about rewarding or punishing behaviour, unidirectional, didactic or indoctrinating. It needs to be based on the cultivation of character virtues such as compassion, honesty, courage, justice, respect and wisdom. This is why this book draws heavily on the research conducted by two of the authors at the Jubilee Centre for Character and Virtues at the University of Birmingham.[6]

In this book we explain the three core components of the Futureproof framework and their six interrelated objectives. We will show educators how to target their approach to digital citizenship education with the goal of enhancing digital flourishing. Put differently, all decisions should be aimed towards digital flourishing, defined as the ability to live well, individually and collectively, in a digital world worth living in. In order for pupils to understand what **digital flourishing** is and why it is important in their own and others' lives, schools must fulfil the following two objectives.

- **Promote a shared digital vision**: pupils need a vision for digital flourishing that informs and helps them to evaluate their use of digital technologies.
- **Promote digital literacy**: pupils need a common language and a functional and critical set of skills and knowledge about digital

technologies that can enable them to use these in ways that contribute to digital flourishing.

We will then show educators how to develop a set of digital rules – these are the principles and guidelines that inform pupils' behaviour and actions to ensure they contribute to digital flourishing, thus outlining a set of minimum expectations on pupils' behaviour. The **digital rules** that schools put in place should meet the following two objectives.

- **Enforce digital policies**: pupils need to adhere to a commonly shaped and agreed set of policies about when digital technologies can be used and for what purpose.
- **Provide guidance on an agreed netiquette**: pupils need to create and adhere to a set of guidelines for using digital technologies and acting online, both individually and in interactions with others, in a way that contributes to human flourishing.

Finally, we will explain that digital character refers to the character qualities that pupils must cultivate and develop if they are to use digital technologies in a way that enables them to avoid or cope with risks while maximising opportunities. Pupils who act with character will have elevated expectations for how they and others should interact when using digital technologies. The building blocks of digital character are the different virtues, the most important of which is digital wisdom, understood as the ability to do the right thing at the right time when using digital technologies. In order to support pupils to develop **digital character**, schools must fulfil the following two objectives.

- **Cultivate digital virtues**: pupils need to possess character qualities that help them and others to flourish digitally.
- **Hone digital wisdom**: pupils need to possess wisdom that enables them to act autonomously, with deliberation and discernment, within different online settings, and that helps them to do the right thing at the right time.

We will come back to these components and objectives at regular intervals throughout the book, as they are at the heart of the Futureproof framework.

OVERVIEW OF THE BOOK

Futureproof aims to be a practical and accessible guide to delivering digital citizenship education. It is a book that we hope readers will dip in and out of as required – we wrote it more as a 'how to' manual than a book that should be read cover to cover.

The book contains four sections:

- **Part 1 provides background information about the framework and why it is needed**. This section will situate the book as well as provide a rationale for it. We recommend that people tasked with adapting and implementing the framework in their school read this whole section in order to gain the big picture and key advice.

- **Part 2 presents the framework – it is the heart of the book**. This is the section that we anticipate will be most thumbed by readers as they adapt the different components of the framework to their particular context. The theory behind each of the three core components (digital flourishing, digital rules, digital character) is explained in a way that makes sense to practitioners. This section includes a step-by-step guide to implementing the framework and is full of activities, resources and case studies that aim to inform and inspire.

- **Part 3 outlines the 10 overarching digital risks and opportunities that the framework addresses**. Each of the risks and opportunities is explained in detail. We provide a definition for each, a background overview of its nature, headlines from key research and sources of further support and advice. Finally, we provide two tables, focusing on learning expectations and related school policies, that link the components and objectives of the framework to the risks and opportunities outlined earlier in this section. As such, part 3 will be useful for readers who want to know, in greater depth, the nature and implications of key digital risks and opportunities, and how the framework can be applied in practice in ways that link to such risks and opportunities.

- **Part 4 explores how to overcome any obstacles that might make implementing the framework challenging**. This includes how to get staff, teachers and parents on board, how to adapt the framework to different settings, how to address issues linked to diversity and how to evaluate whether the framework has an impact. Each part contains an introduction to orient readers and allow them to dip in and out. Key themes and lessons are highlighted throughout.

THE PATH TO DIGITAL FLOURISHING

As a group of authors, we each bring different yet complementary skills, experience and qualifications to the book. Two of us (Tom and Gianfranco) work in a university, have PhDs in the field of digital education, and spend most of our time researching the impact of digital technologies on children and society more broadly. Two of us (Sophie and Lee) work in schools at the coalface of delivering digital citizenship education, experiencing first-hand the opportunities and risks that living in the digital age presents to pupils today. We have all witnessed, through our research and first-hand experience, how much the inventions of the smartphone, laptop, tablet and other technologies have impacted (for good and bad) the lives of children and young people. Despite our different backgrounds, we were united by a single aim when we agreed to write this book: to help teachers help their pupils to maximise the opportunities and minimise the risks of living in the digital age.

We had several hopes when we began writing. We really hoped teachers would find the book useful and, dare we say, inspiring. At the very least, we hoped it would help those teachers wondering what to 'do' about digital citizenship education to think more strategically about their approach. Ultimately, we hoped the book would encourage teachers to stop and think about their current practice, and consider what needs to be done to ensure their pupils are prepared for their futures.

We understand that implementing this new framework will be an ambitious aim. It will take some upheaval and change. It will most definitely take thought and planning. However, given that pupils' lives – and, in fact, most of our lives – are increasingly hybrid these days, we think the time and effort necessary to implement the framework will ultimately be worth it. The path to digital flourishing is ongoing but we all have a responsibility to help pupils make a start on it.

PART 1

INTRODUCING THE DIGITAL CITIZENSHIP FRAMEWORK

THE GAP

Given that all schools, in some form, teach digital citizenship, a reasonable question might be: why do we need a new framework? The simple and perhaps surprising answer is that there is no popular framework in the UK that details a comprehensive approach to education for digital citizenship for four- to 16-year-olds.

The approach that many schools adopt to prepare pupils for their digital lives and futures might best be described as somewhat ad hoc. This does not mean that current teaching about issues related to digital technologies is not of a high standard. A typical school might have a PSHE teacher who gives a thought-provoking series of lessons on cyberbullying every year, a computing teacher who inspires pupils to try coding, and a headteacher who gives an annual assembly on online privacy that gets pupils thinking and talking. These, on their own, are valuable and important lessons for pupils to learn. Yet they could be so much more powerful if they were part of a planned, coordinated and conscious strategy to educate pupils about digital risks and opportunities. This is the aim of the Futureproof framework: to inform a whole-school approach to digital citizenship education that is not reactive and that deals simply with the issues of the moment, while preparing pupils for the digital lives they lead in and beyond school.

Such a planned, comprehensive and reflective approach to education for digital citizenship would require school leaders, teachers, pupils, parents, governors, members of the school community and other interested parties to come together and answer the following questions.

- How do schools teach pupils about digital risks and opportunities in a balanced way?

- How are pupils prepared for their digital futures through explicit (taught) activities that are supported through the culture, values and ethos of the school?

- How do specific lessons on topics such as AI link to drop-down days on employability, or to assemblies about online learning?

- How do school rules and guidelines about the use of digital technologies link to longer-term aspirations to cultivate character in pupils, so they use these technologies wisely when they leave school?

- What is the overarching goal of education about digital technology, and how does this link to pupils viewing themselves as local, national and global citizens?

- Are rules about technology use in schools applied consistently, and do pupils and staff understand how and why those rules have been developed and implemented?

- Do pupils leave school with elements of a deeper knowledge about aspects of digital technologies, and are they aware of how these aspects link together?

It is these questions and others that this book addresses. Schools that apply the framework can be confident they are providing their pupils with a joined-up and far-reaching education for digital citizenship. For some schools, this might mean unpicking and reorganising current practice, or even starting over again. This should be an urgent task, given how important it is that pupils leave school with the knowledge, skills, competencies and character required to flourish in the digital world.

BUILDING ON WHAT IS ALREADY AVAILABLE

Despite the lack of a cohesive and comprehensive framework, education for digital citizenship is important and highly regarded by educators. As detailed in the table below, there are a number of statutory and non-statutory requirements and guidelines relating to digital citizenship education to which schools must adhere. In the table, we list the most important publications from the UK government and other organisations, and explain what their strengths are and how those strengths complement our advice in this book.

Publication	Description	How it complements the advice in *Futureproof*
Education for a Connected World (2020)	Published by the UK Council for Internet Safety, this publication is a tool to inform the development of teaching and learning, aimed at supporting children and young people to live knowledgeably, responsibly and safely in the digital world.	Focuses mainly on digital risks (and the skills and knowledge required to avoid or cope with these risks) in relation, for example, to cyberbullying, privacy, security and managing information online. Relatedly, it provides a detailed metric of what pupils should know about internet safety at different ages (see part 3 of *Futureproof*). Useful for developing a rich, effective and developmental curriculum that will support pupils to be safe, healthy and thriving online (part 3). Useful for auditing and evaluating existing provision of internet safety education (part 4). Has the potential to inform the development of effective training for school staff and governors/ board members (part 4).

Publication	Description	How it complements the advice in *Futureproof*
Teaching Online Safety in School (2019)	Published by the Department for Education, this non-statutory guidance supports schools to teach pupils how to stay safe online in the context of studying new and existing subjects.	Focuses primarily on digital risks and pupils' wellbeing (part 3). Details how to support vulnerable pupils (part 4). Recommends a whole-school approach to internet safety (part 1).
Relationships Education, Relationships and Sex Education (RSE) and Health Education (2019)	Published by the DfE, this is statutory guidance for primary and secondary schools on relationships education, RSE and health education. Many of the issues addressed in the guidance relate to pupils' lives online.	Is statutory and details the digital risks that schools must teach about, and how to avoid or cope with these (part 3).
Online Harms White Paper (2019)	Proposed by the Department for Digital, Culture, Media and Sport and the Home Office, this is a bill progressing through Parliament that primarily outlines a new regulatory framework to improve citizens' safety online. One of its sections focuses on the responsibilities of educators to help individuals feel empowered and manage their own safety online.	Links to the development of digital literacy, referred to as 'online media literacy' (part 2 – objective 2). Focuses primarily on legislation (part 2 – objective 3). Details likely new legislation that will inform how schools can support the reduction of online harms. This includes changes to school curriculum content – in computing, for example (part 3).
Online Media Literacy Strategy (2021)	Designed by the DCMS, this is a publication that, in line with the goals set out in the *Online Harms White Paper*, outlines a framework for promoting digital literacy among the general public.	Outlines five principles that detail the skills and knowledge users should possess when using the internet (part 2 – objectives 2 and 5). Focuses on the importance of evaluating online content and of understanding the broader digital environment and its implications for privacy (parts 2 and 3). Suggests that users' online interactions should be underpinned by an understanding of the consequences of their actions, of digital risks and of how to positively contribute to and participate in society (part 2 – objective 5).

Publication	Description	How it complements the advice in *Futureproof*
Growing Up Digital (2017)	Published by the Children's Commissioner for England, this publication provides guidance on how to create a supportive digital environment for children.	Focuses on how children can be supported to be resilient, informed and empowered when using the internet (part 2 – objective 5). Details what changes could be made to the school curriculum, such as in computing, to ensure that children develop the skills and knowledge they need to be resilient and act as responsible citizens online (part 1). Outlines five key rights that children should have when using the internet: the right to remove their online content; the right to know who has access to their data; the right to safety and support; the right to informed and conscious use of the internet; and the right to digital literacy (part 2 – objectives 3 and 4).

These publications are complemented by many excellent and easily accessible digital citizenship lessons and resources. In 2021, a search of the following terms on the Tes resources platform for secondary school teachers resulted in the following hits: digital citizenship, 1,041; fake news, 481; cyberbullying, 320; trolling, 100; revenge porn, 29.[7] Tes is just one of many sites in the UK that teachers turn to when looking for inspiration. There are also many charities and organisations that offer advice, support and educational resources (such as Common Sense, the UK Safer Internet Centre, Childnet and the National Crime Agency's Child Exploitation and Online Protection Command).

Academics have published books and articles that discuss evidence-based approaches to addressing online harms through education. For example, Marilyn Campbell and Sheri Bauman have edited a book reviewing 13 international evidence-based programmes that have been found to reduce cyberbullying.[8] Other researchers have published frameworks for digital citizenship. Perhaps the best known is that proposed by Mike Ribble, who suggests nine components of digital citizenship.[9] The International Society for Technology in Education also advises of nine digital citizenship components,[10] and the iKeepSafe organisation recommends five components required for digital safety.[11] In addition to these publications, government agencies and departments have published reports about online harms that make recommendations for educational practice. These have not, as yet, translated into clear advice from the Department for Education, which currently encourages schools to develop their own curricula by taking guidance from organisations such as the PSHE Association. There is even less guidance in the citizenship education curriculum, where the focus tends to be on digital forms of political literacy and online social action.

The plethora of advice, support and resources is enough to make teachers' heads spin as they seek to develop coordinated approaches to education for digital citizenship that are evidence-based and respond to the ethical concerns of the digital age. In the absence of consistent guidance, many schools are left to develop their own approaches to digital citizenship.

The framework that we propose takes inspiration from many of these lessons, resources and previous frameworks, and shows how they can be bound together so teachers in any school can give pupils a coherent message about how to best navigate the challenges and possibilities associated with their current and future digital lives. The framework does not dismiss the many resources that are available; rather, it provides a frame to organise and hang them on. It provides some order and structure, which in turn can ensure there is some consistency in meaning, purpose and practice. The aim of the framework is to help teachers and pupils make sense of their digital lives and provide them with the knowledge that is most pertinent to them.

IT'S NOT JUST TEACHERS' RESPONSIBILITY

Although we wrote this book with teachers in mind, we want to make it very clear from the outset that we do not think digital citizenship education is teachers' responsibility alone – far from it. Likewise, we do not think that being a 'good' digital citizen is the sole responsibility of pupils. To start with, they have been dealt a challenging hand. To grow up in the digital world presents children and young people with challenges that many adults never faced. This is largely due to the tech companies and the way digital technologies have been developed. Many other books have been written about big tech companies and ethics, and we do not have space to delve into these now. Suffice to say, we understand that when tech is driven by business alone, human flourishing will suffer. This has led to our pupils playing in a digital playground that is full of tricky obstacles. We should not be over-moralising about children's behaviour online for this very reason – all of us are learning how best to live with others in the digital age and very few of us have never made mistakes. When many adults and stakeholders, including tech developers and distributors, have been found to act in ways that may be morally questionable, we should understand how challenging it may be for children and young people to use digital technologies.

Our hope is that the tech designers of the future (many of whom are in teachers' classrooms today) will help. They will seek to create new technologies in ways that promote value-driven design and will think more carefully about the possible impact of these technologies on individual and societal flourishing. This might even include inventing technologies that contribute to character and values education – technologies that would be a great help to teachers today.

We also understand that parents and policymakers have considerable responsibilities. Policymakers can help by ensuring that digital citizenship education is prioritised in schools, and support schools in ensuring that they have sufficient time and sufficiently experienced teachers to teach it successfully. Parents, meanwhile, are ultimately responsible for their children's behaviour. They should be the ones who first react if their children are found to be bullying or hurting people online. In part 4 of this book, we discuss how parents and teachers might work together in the context of delivering digital citizenship education. There is much more that can be said about how teachers should not be battling alone at the frontline of ensuring an ethical digital age, but we will leave those arguments for previous (see Tom Harrison's book for parents, *Thrive*[12]) and future publications. For now, our main point is that teachers have a responsibility for digital citizenship education, and we hope this book will help educators in this respect.

WHY THE FRAMEWORK WILL HELP SCHOOLS

It is perhaps not surprising that many schools do not take a joined-up approach to providing digital citizenship education. Digital technologies have changed rapidly over the past 20 years and schools, on the whole, have struggled to keep up. In most cases, they (like all of us) have had to react to the invention and widespread use of personal computers, tablets and smartphones. Schools are still working out how artificial intelligence, virtual reality and the internet, among other interventions, might impact on them for the better or for the worse. In the early 2000s, many schools integrated lessons on cyberbullying in PSHE when online abuse started to become a problem. Similarly, they started to teach about social media and democracy in the early 2010s after the uprisings in the Middle East that are commonly referred to as the Arab Spring. In short, schools' approaches to digital citizenship education might be described as organic – lessons and topics are added to the school calendar as new issues emerge. This will continue to be the case unless school leaders stop reacting to developments in digital technologies and try to get ahead of the game.

Given the current milieu, we argue in this book that a new approach is required for the following four reasons.

1. DIGITAL TECHNOLOGIES PROVIDE OPPORTUNITIES FOR PUPILS LIVING IN THE DIGITAL WORLD

Digital technologies might be viewed as the unsung hero of the Covid-19 pandemic. Among many other things, they helped parents to educate their children at home, scientists to share information quickly around the world, and children and adults to continue learning and working remotely, while also providing opportunities for social interaction and entertainment during lockdown. Nevertheless, some books on digital technologies can be apocalyptic, making wild arguments about technologies destroying humanity. These types of books add to a moral panic. Moral panics are not, on the whole, helpful. When we are panicking, we do not necessarily think objectively or rationally. We do not consider both sides of the story. We do not tend to make sound decisions.

Our belief, as many others would put it, is that technology can be part of the solution to the issues that we currently worry about. Technology can bring us together to work on joint global problems, allowing us to collaborate on issues such as the environment, how to respond effectively and efficiently to future pandemics, and how to promote causes of social justice and advance democracy.

In *Futureproof*, we remain positive about the potential of technologies to help individuals and the world to flourish. This is not based on blind optimism, but hard evidence that, when technologies are used in a way that furthers humanity, the ends are generally positive. We think that perhaps some of the early adopters of the internet were a bit too wide-eyed; we trusted the slogans and our fingers were burned. As Rana Foroohar argues in her book *Don't Be Evil*[13] (which was Google's early slogan), many of the internet pioneers 'lost their soul' along the way. This was largely, we believe, in the pursuit of market value (and share) over human values (and care). Other pioneers such as Tim Berners-Lee, the inventor of the World Wide Web, still hold up a light that the internet – and the many technologies that rely on it – can be essentially positive. Writing an open letter on the 30th anniversary of the technology he invented, Sir Tim wrote:

> ... *given how much the web has changed in the past 30 years, it would be defeatist and unimaginative to assume that the web as we know it can't be changed for the better in the next 30. If we give up on building a better web now, then the web will not have failed us. We will have failed the web ... The web is for everyone and collectively we hold the power to change it. It won't be easy. But if we dream a little and work a lot, we can get the web we want.*[14]

We think we need to channel some of this positive thought, and we see our efforts to educate pupils to live well with digital technologies as part of the solution. We can perhaps view the past couple of decades as a chance to learn and see what works and what does not. The pupils we educate today will be the tech inventors and leaders of the future; the qualities and values they hold will inform how they carry out these roles. It is therefore important that we remain positive and hopeful, and maintain a belief that how we teach pupils today will have a long-term impact on the world.

2. DIGITAL TECHNOLOGIES PRESENT RISKS TO PUPILS LIVING IN THE DIGITAL WORLD

The benefits that digital technologies bring to our lives are often underappreciated. This is, in part, down to their perceived negative impact on our wellbeing, morality and overall human flourishing. There is no getting away from these often serious concerns – they are a genuine and all-too-real blight on many children's (and adults') lives. The early internet pioneers had high hopes that the internet would revolutionise the world as well as improve it. Their first hope has undoubtedly been realised, but we are a long way off realising their second.

The detrimental effects of living in the digital age have been well documented. The list of 'social ills' attributed to new and emerging technologies is long and growing. These include, to name a few, concern at the rise of online incivility, fake news and misinformation damaging trust,[15] the so-called rise of 'evil online',[16] malevolent subcultures on the dark net,[17] and a decoupling of scientific and technical advancement from democratic advancement.[18] These headline concerns sometimes mask the real and everyday issues that teachers are expected to deal with, such as cyberbullying, online plagiarism, misinformation, online harassment, trolling and sexting.

The nature of morality in the digital age has been dealt with in numerous publications. The debate can be divided between those who promote the internet as largely a force for good, those who see it as morally corrupting and those who present a more balanced view. We think there is some truth in all these accounts, and which one teachers believe will depend on how digital technologies impact on them and their pupils. Given the prevalence and potential severity of online harms and the challenges they present to flourishing, it is incumbent on teachers (alongside parents, governments, tech companies and individuals themselves) to address this issue. This reason itself does not provide a prima facie case for a *new* framework for teaching digital citizenship – just the need for a framework to guide practice. After all, many of these issues are similar to those found offline, just in a different form.

3. THE AFFORDANCES OF THE INTERNET MEAN WE CANNOT ADOPT TRADITIONAL APPROACHES TO ADDRESSING ONLINE HARMS RESULTING FROM THE USE OF DIGITAL TECHNOLOGIES

What has become clear is that the internet provides pupils with affordances[19] that can affect their behaviour. The ability to communicate instantly at any time in any place, to interact anonymously and to avoid rules means that many people can behave differently online to how they would in person. What is less clear is whether this different behaviour is intentional or not. There is a convincing line of argument that our judgements are clouded when we interact in ways that are digitally mediated – we are not always clear on what the 'right' thing to do is. Shannon Vallor calls this a 'moral fog'.[20] Our normative expectations about what we say and do have somehow changed online and we do not know what the new rules are. This is perhaps one reason why there is a rise in online trolling, hate speech and other divisive communication online.

It is because of the affordances of the internet, which can have an impact on users' behaviour, that we need a new framework for teaching digital citizenship. We cannot simply assume that older and more traditional approaches to character education, citizenship education and PSHE will be sufficient for teaching about the internet, online harms and the constantly evolving challenges that digital technologies present. We need to think again, starting with understanding the day-to-day realities of pupils' lives today, as well as what their realities might look like in the future.

Let us make the case by listing some of the affordances we think have affected the way that many users, including pupils, tend to interact online.

- The internet (at least in the Western world) is designed and managed in ways that maximise freedom of expression through connectivity, interactivity and the possibility of not just accessing but also producing and sharing information. Although this is one of the strengths of the internet, it often translates as a reduced sense of rules, monitoring and enforcement, which creates an impression – and is indicative – of the extent to which digitally mediated interactions are often under-regulated. This is why, for example, school bullies think they are less likely to be caught online than offline.

- It is easier to communicate with others anonymously using digital technologies. Users can set up fake accounts, use fake profile pictures or set up false identities to avoid detection and therefore accountability for their actions. This is one reason why there are so many scams online, as criminals feel safe hidden behind their computer screens.

- Digital communication is often imperfect. Although we increasingly use video calls, most of our digital communications occur through the written word: texts, emails, social media posts, etc. Without body language and other visual clues, children and young people are not faced with the immediate emotional response that might make them check or change their behaviour. How individuals act offline is mediated by those around them – a smile or a frown can make them change their behaviour. When these visual cues are missing, their actions are guided more by their own thoughts, feelings and emotions. A great deal of research shows that a decrease in 'social presence' can reduce empathy and feelings of guilt.[21]

- The line between online and offline is increasingly blurred. When pupils used to go home at the end of a school day, they could use the evening to reflect and talk through with their parents any issues they had faced at school. While this is still possible today, it is increasingly harder for them to disconnect from the online world, as they are constantly prompted to use apps, social media platforms and other online services, whether to play games or communicate with friends. As a result, it may be harder for them to take time, pause and think through issues, as communication has become more immediate, fleeting and ubiquitous in the digital age.

Of course, most of the affordances provided by the internet and other digital technologies can be used for benign as well as toxic purposes, and are also the reason why they are popular.[22] Relatedly, these affordances are one of the reasons why we need a new framework for teaching digital citizenship education, in order to deal with the ways in which digital technologies have impacted on society, taking into account the changes in how we interact and behave with each other online. It could be argued that all that is required is for curricula and lessons to be updated to reflect the changes brought about by digital technologies. We think that such tinkering might have some positive effect, but given the importance of digital technologies to children's and young people's future lives, we should not teach about these technologies in silos. The affordances brought by digital technologies to pupils are significant enough to warrant a whole-school approach. The Futureproof framework responds to these affordances, showing how we can teach children and young people to use digital technologies to enhance rather than negatively impact on human flourishing.

4. WE MUST START WITH A THEORETICALLY BASED FRAMEWORK AS WE CANNOT YET RELY ON EMPIRICAL DATA TO SHOW US THE WAY

A justification for proposing a mainly theoretically based framework for delivering digital citizenship education is that, at the present time, empirical research cannot tell us exactly which digital educational practices do or do not work. There is currently a paucity of quality and/ or comprehensive research in the field. This does not mean there is not a great deal of excellent research going on, including trials of educational interventions and exploratory and action research. What we have right now are some really good jigsaw pieces, but no research can tell us yet what the full picture looks like. We must, for the present time, rely on well-considered theory.

The pace of technological change has left research into its impact on human flourishing trailing behind. We simply do not have reliable data about how the internet impacts on human morality, or how education should respond. In 2019, Amy Orben and Andrew Przybylski published detailed research using large data sets to investigate the links between adolescence, wellbeing and digital technology use.[23] They showed how easy it is, when running the data, to find headline-worthy results. However, many of their analyses produced what are known as false positives – if the data were to be analysed again, a different result would probably be found.

Orben and Przybylski showed that it is almost impossible at the present time to make conclusive claims about how digital technology use impacts on wellbeing. Their findings are perhaps not surprising given the many well-known limitations associated with studying the field. Few studies are impervious to claims against their validity. Limitations include: trying to make inferences about individuals from vast population-wide data sets; the challenge of keeping up with new, omnipresent technologies that are often superseded before there is time to study them properly, leading to a lack of longitudinal studies; and a reliance on self-reported data – studies based on children telling about their use of the internet that likely contain some bias.

Because empirical research cannot, as yet, tell us what we need to do, we must draw on evidence to some extent, while relying on theory to provide a digital citizenship education framework for overarching practice. Although there are some helpful studies that support particular interventions targeting particular issues, there is no research that supports an overarching and intentional approach to educating for digital citizenship. For now, practitioners must draw on data when this is deemed helpful and fill in the gaps with well-considered theory.

We have outlined the four reasons above in order to make the case for the new framework we propose in this book. In summary, we need a framework to guide a whole-school approach to digital citizenship education in schools for the following reasons.

- We must recognise the many possibilities that digital technologies bring pupils today and are likely to bring in the future.
- We must recognise the risks that digital technologies bring pupils today and are likely to bring in the future.
- We must recognise that the affordances associated with digital technologies change the way we interact and behave.
- We must recognise that, currently, research cannot tell us comprehensively what does or does not work in this area, which is why we need a theoretically based framework to guide practice.

Schools should recognise that many excellent resources and sources of advice are available that respond to these issues and guide practice. What is lacking, we argue, is an overarching guiding frame around which to organise these resources in a way that makes sense and adds meaning for pupils and teachers. The Futureproof framework provides the scaffolding around which the practices currently available can be organised, while also exposing any gaps in those practices.

FUTUREPROOF

Calling a book *Futureproof* is perhaps a bold move. How can we be confident that the approach to digital citizenship education that we propose today will prepare pupils for their lives in 10, 20 or 50 years' time? Our confidence is based on the following two reasons.

- In the framework, we focus on digital opportunities and risks. Currently, much digital citizenship education is reactive and responds to risks as they arise. This can lead to a narrowing of focus to the present and teachers running around firefighting. Looking at digital opportunities in tandem with digital risks enables us to better reflect on the future.

- By using a virtue ethical lens (see page 53), we are putting our confidence in the development of character over rules. As we have found to our detriment, it is very hard to impose rules and regulations in the digital world. Many of the issues we face today are the result of how technologies have developed, and it is challenging to retrofit rules to manage them. This is largely because it is difficult to predict what rules might be needed before the impact of new technology has been determined. The move to a focus on character is therefore attractive, as character by its very nature is situation-dependent. We do not know what new technology will look like, but we know people will still need courage, wisdom, compassion, honesty and other qualities to make and use it.

Our roles as academics and teachers on the frontline teaching digital citizenship have allowed us to consider immediate and future concerns alongside each other. We have tried to consider how what is happening today will affect the future. We have tried to record what lessons can be learned from our digital lives to date, and how these can inform what we might do differently in the future. Twenty years after digital technologies became ever-present in most of our lives is a great time to take stock, to think about what we might do differently, and to make plans that prepare for the future and do not simply deal with the present. We have observed and taken advice from research, and spoken with teachers, pupils and parents to envisage what a new overarching approach might look like.

Our aspiration for *Futureproof* is based on a simple (yet difficult to achieve) premise: that technology is beneficial when it enhances humanity. We want current and emerging digital technologies to be of value to humans in the future and to help solve global issues that are likely to become increasingly pressing. To ensure tech is part of the solution, we have to ensure that pupils can deal with the risks presented by digital technologies and maximise their opportunities. Pupils should be encouraged to think about how values might be designed into new technologies, and about why future inventions should not be designed solely with profit in mind but also with a view to how they might contribute to the common good.

In the process of writing *Futureproof*, we have sought to anticipate the future of pupils who are entering primary school today, in order to:

- Anticipate how digital technologies will be increasingly present in every aspect of their lives. For example, we are only on the cusp of what some would refer to as the AI revolution. Google has predicted that, in time, AI will be more important to humanity than the discovery of fire.

- Demonstrate that character will increasingly matter as rule-making and enforcement cannot keep pace with technology.

- Encourage pupils – and in fact all of us – to be open-minded about the possibilities of digital technologies and about how technology has and will continue to have benefits, as well as changing how we do things (for good or bad).

- Understand that we all need to develop resilience and an ability to adapt in order to deal with constant changes.

WHAT IS DIGITAL CITIZENSHIP EDUCATION?

The term 'citizenship' commonly refers to the legal status or membership of a nation state. On this reading, a citizen is an individual recognised in law as enjoying certain rights and possessing certain responsibilities. Understood more broadly, citizenship involves active engagement within one's own communities, contributing to these morally; as such, citizenship is a contested and multi-layered concept. Citizenship education in the UK has tended to focus more on the rights and responsibilities of citizens, as opposed to their legal status. The citizenship education curriculum, building on the original vision for the subject from Bernard Crick (a prominent political theorist), has traditionally focused on three interlinked areas: political literacy, community involvement and morally good action. Our framework for digital citizenship education covers all these areas and more.

Digital citizenship is often understood as the following of 'norms of appropriate, responsible behaviour' in the context of interacting with others and participating in society in ways that are digitally mediated.[24] Such an understanding of digital citizenship might be criticised by those who draw on critical theory and take a more politicised view of the concept as embedded within systemic inequalities.[25] They might be rightly concerned that digital citizenship is about strong and powerful groups or individuals telling others what to do and how to behave online. We want to state emphatically that this is not the case with the Futureproof framework. Our framework does not seek to extend existing power structures. Rather, it has due regard for individual autonomy and critical expression.

Having defined what we mean by digital citizenship, we will now explain what we mean by 'digital citizenship education'.

At its simplest, digital citizenship education is any form of teaching and learning directed at helping pupils to flourish in the digital world. It is related to similar terms including e-citizenship, online citizenship and cyber-citizenship, and is taught in some form in most primary and secondary schools in the UK. Different schools and other educational settings use the term in a variety of ways, and it has become a catch-all term to describe learning directed at, among others, the following topics: online safety, cyberbullying, online harms, online democracy, online volunteering, privacy and digital footprint. These issues and topics are normally covered in the UK as part of the PSHE, citizenship and/or computing curricula. Lessons are complemented with whole-school activities, including communications with parents, assemblies, invited speakers and drop-down days on particular topics. The Futureproof framework includes all these topics and approaches, and brings a coordinated, planned, whole-school approach to the task of educating for digital citizenship.

In this book, digital citizenship education covers all of the following:

- Education that focuses on the risks and opportunities brought about by digital technologies.
- Education that helps pupils to use digital technologies now and in the future.
- Implicit and explicit attempts to teach pupils to use digital technologies wisely.
- Education beyond the classroom. Although this is important, implicit or explicit learning can be reinforced, almost by osmosis, by being part of a school culture and ethos and living within a school community.
- Education that relates to what it means to be a citizen of a country or place, but is more about a way of being.
- Education that is not about telling pupils how to behave, or forcing them to behave as good citizens, but encourages them to think deeply and reflectively about how they want to live in their digital world.

There is no single, foolproof approach to digital citizenship education that will work for all pupils in all situations. School leaders and teachers need to adapt approaches to fit the context of their school and the needs of individual pupils. Digital citizenship education must be made relevant to pupils and they must find it accessible – meaningful to their lives and their circumstances. For example, schools serving pupils from more disadvantaged backgrounds should recognise that many of the pupils they serve will not have the same digital opportunities. In part 4 of this book, we discuss ways for educators to ensure the framework is inclusive and reflects the realities of life for pupils from diverse backgrounds.

TERMINOLOGY USED IN THE BOOK

The terminology related to digital technology can be a semantic minefield, so it is important that we are clear from the outset of this book what we mean by the various terms we use. We try, as far as possible, to use terms that are common in schools as well as in broader society, but a closer look reveals that there is often confusion about this terminology. For example, 'digital' and 'online' are sometimes used interchangeably, although they mean different things.

Throughout the book, we predominantly use the prefix 'digital' unless we are referring to a risk or opportunity that only presents itself online. In its most literal sense, 'digital' refers to the use of binary code, which is based on the use of the digits 0 and 1. We use the term more broadly to show that many of the risks and opportunities that affect pupils now and in the future are not just about children and young people living and interacting online, but also arise from the development of new and emerging digital technologies. The key point is that by using the term 'digital technologies', we wish to convey the idea that our framework for delivering digital citizenship education is broader than just the technologies that use the internet. Although many of the risks that digital technologies present for children are linked to the internet, the current and future opportunities that we must educate pupils about are linked to the use of digital technologies more broadly, in ways that may or may not necessarily rely on the internet. Furthermore, a truly futureproof framework must cultivate in pupils character qualities that can anticipate the challenges inherent in using digital technologies that have yet to be invented.

The following table presents the key terms that we use in this book.

Term	Definition
Digital citizenship education	Any form of formal or informal teaching and learning that is directed at helping pupils to use digital technologies to positively benefit their own and others' lives.
Digital technologies	Any electronic devices or systems that pupils knowingly or unknowingly use to access, create, store, share or process data and information. This broad definition includes hardware such as smartphones, laptops, computers and tablets, as well as software including communication apps, social media and online games. It also includes emerging technologies such as artificial intelligence (AI), machine learning, virtual reality (VR), blockchain and the internet of things, which refers to the network of devices around the world connected to the internet.
Digital risks	Threats and dangers posed to children and young people now and in the future from their own or others' use of digital technologies.
Digital opportunities	A favourable activity or experience that children and young people can access through their own and others' use of digital technologies.
Digital flourishing	Individual and collective happiness and wellbeing that comes from living well in a digital world worth living in.
Digital rules	The policies, guidelines and rules that a school must put in place to help pupils maximise digital opportunities and minimise digital risks.
Digital character	Character qualities, virtues (or values) and strengths that ensure pupils can live wisely in the present and future digital world.

DIGITAL RISKS AND OPPORTUNITIES

As previously stated, the digital world brings risks and opportunities for children and young people. Those who write about what we should do about these risks and opportunities can be broadly split into three categories.

1. **Non-interventionists** believe, to a greater or lesser extent, that it is not primarily the job of educators to 'teach' children how to use digital technologies, and that children should be given the freedom to learn this experientially. This view is captured, first and foremost, by Don Tapscott's seminal 1997 book *Growing Up Digital*, which celebrates the potential of the internet to enable children to play a more active role in the ways in which they think, learn, play and communicate. In his book, Tapscott predicted a moral panic about digital technologies, suggesting that 'concerns about the Internet, by cynics, moralists or technophobes, are plain wrong'.[26] Since then his views have been replicated by others, including, most recently, Jordan Shapiro, who argues in his book *The New Childhood* that we, as a society, need to embrace digital technologies, and that fear and nostalgia are powerful enemies that stand in the way of children's best interests.[27] Likewise, in his book *Lost in a Good Game*, Pete Etchells condemns scaremongering and moral panics about online gaming.[28]

Interestingly, the non-interventionist position is posited on practical and ideological grounds. Practically speaking, and perhaps quite reasonably, it is rooted in the recognition that many parents and teachers were not 'born digital' and often do not have the skills or experience to 'teach' young people how to use new and emerging technologies.[29] This gap became particularly apparent during the Covid-19 crisis, when some teachers struggled to move their teaching online. Indeed, irrespective of whether scholars do or do not take such a position, it is often argued in the literature that a generational knowledge gap exists between adults and children – one that has turned the tables, when it comes to technology, on traditional hierarchical relationships between teachers and students.[30] The non-interventionist position of scholars like Shapiro is built around this argument. This position champions the role of children as learning agents in ways that resonate with the cyber-libertarian ethos that characterises the advent of the internet and current discourses about the digital environment – discourses that prioritise individual liberty on social, political and economic levels.[31]

2. **Interventionists** believe, to a greater or lesser extent, that we cannot simply leave children and young people to their own devices – we must help them to grow up digitally savvy. So-called interventionists are generally less positive about the impact of the internet on children's and young people's lives and morality, and use anecdotes and evidence to support their claims. Presenting a particularly visceral image of what they call the 'many faces of evil online', Dean Cocking and Jeroen van den Hoven describe the worst aspects of the internet in unflinching terms throughout their book *Evil Online*.[32] This includes anecdotes, both alarming and moving, about cyberbullying, trolling, online humiliation, revenge porn and other forms of online abuse.

Meanwhile, others have taken more empirical approaches to make their case, citing statistics that show the prevalence of online abuse and issues such as online plagiarism and piracy to demonstrate the ill effects of the internet on humanity.[33] These have been used as the basis for a slew of policy documents in the UK about the possible impact of the internet on children's and young people's wellbeing, mental health and overall potential to flourish in the digital age.[34] From this perspective, policymakers are expected to actively intervene – from regulating online platforms to promoting internet safety education – with a view to protecting children and young people from the risks of the online world. It is important to note, nevertheless, that many large dataset studies that show links between the internet, moral wrongdoing, young people and wellbeing have been challenged on empirical grounds.[35]

3. **Pragmatists** believe, to a greater or lesser extent, that the digital age brings risks and opportunities for children and young people. We would put ourselves in this group. Much has been written about digital risks and opportunities since Sonia Livingstone first bought our attention to these terms in her 2009 book *Children and the Internet*.[36] Commentators such as Livingstone have attempted to go beyond polarising accounts of the impact of digital technologies on children and young people. They strive for a more balanced argument that children need, on the one hand, to be protected from online risks and, on the other hand, to be encouraged to pursue online opportunities. Such an approach suggests that a balance between protecting and empowering children in terms of how they use the internet is essential. For pragmatists, making a distinction between risks and opportunities is the easier task. However, drawing a line between when and how to intervene or not is less easy. Our framework for digital citizenship education aims to help teachers with this task.

Futureproof is written for pragmatists who understand that:

- The digital age brings some problematic risks but also considerable potential benefits for pupils (and for society at large).
- These risks and opportunities change over time.
- Education can help pupils to maximise digital opportunities and make them less likely to be exposed to, and more likely to be able to cope with, digital risks.
- Pupils are more likely to respond to approaches that deliver digital citizenship education if these show them how to understand and best navigate digital risks and opportunities.

Taking a pragmatic approach, this book recognises, in equal measure, the risks and opportunities that digital technologies present for children and young people. Although these might be split in a multitude of ways, *Futureproof* focuses on 10 overarching areas relating to five risks, which include in turn a number of issues, and five opportunities.

DIGITAL RISKS

Risk	Definition	Issues
Abuse	The use of digital technologies to abuse others.	Cyberbullying, image-based sexual abuse, trolling.
Crime	The use of digital technologies to commit crime.	Online grooming, extremism, theft/fraud/scams/phishing.
Privacy	The use of digital technologies to invade and exploit others' privacy.	Data-tracking, digital footprint.
Mistrust	The use of digital technologies to increase mistrust in society.	Misinformation, distorted identities, plagiarism.
Wellbeing	The use of digital technologies in a way that reduces the mental and/or physical wellbeing of users.	Screen time, inappropriate content, depression and self-harm.

DIGITAL OPPORTUNITIES

Opportunity	Definition
Learning	The use of digital technologies to enhance learning.
Connection	The use of digital technologies to make new connections and develop constructive relationships.
Leisure	The use of digital technologies to express creativity and pursue opportunities of leisure and entertainment.
Employment	The use of digital technologies to further employment and career opportunities.
Citizenship	The use of digital technologies to enhance democratic and civic participation.

Under each of these areas relating to digital risks and opportunities we have selected topics that are of most pressing concern to teachers, parents, children and policymakers today. In doing so, we have made a judgement and chosen those that are pertinent now and are likely to be so for the foreseeable future. We believe that issues related to risks such as cyberbullying are unlikely to go away in the short term, and teachers will be looking for the best ways to educate children about their digital futures for many years to come. In this sense, we hope that the overarching areas we have identified as relating to digital risks and opportunities are to some extent futureproof.

TEACHERS' KNOWLEDGE: DIFFERENTIATING FORM FROM CONTENT

Given the bewildering array of advice, it is perhaps not surprising that many teachers are left in a fog about what to 'do'. They have a dilemma. Do they act as interventionists – and if so, to what extent – by educating children and young people to avoid experiencing and perpetuating digital risks? Or should they stand back and let children and young people experiment freely online and learn by themselves in the process? This dilemma is why we suggest that teachers should act as pragmatists and look beyond simple interpretations of the digital risks versus opportunities debate. However, adopting this viewpoint does not in itself show teachers what they could do to deliver digital citizenship education in ways that are comprehensive and can reach all pupils. *Futureproof* provides practical advice on how to manage this.

Even armed with this practical advice, teachers are still likely to be wary about 'teaching' in a field in which they do not feel they have technical proficiency. Pupils today, perhaps simplistically, have been called 'digital natives'. Building on Marc Prensky's terminology,[37] it is often assumed that, because pupils are born in the digital world, they are proficient in using digital technologies. Meanwhile, many teachers will perhaps categorise themselves as 'digital immigrants' – they were not born into this world and some are therefore understandably fearful of it, or at least concerned about their knowledge of how to use digital technologies. Although the 'native' and 'immigrant' distinction is not particularly nuanced or representative of most schools, it is helpful to think broadly about what knowledge teachers need in order to implement the Futureproof framework. We have constructed the framework so that teachers do not have to be proficient users of technologies to be able to implement it.

To show why this is the case, we will borrow language from art critics to make a distinction between **form** and **content**. Here, 'form' refers to the technology while 'content' refers to the information that circulates through this technology. It is our contention that we can largely leave pupils to learn (often through experimentation and self-teaching) how to use digital technologies practically. This does not mean that we should not teach computing in schools, rather that this teaching should be geared towards encouraging pupils not only to gain digital skills and an understanding of the affordances of digital technologies, but also to develop and create new and ethical technologies. We can, we argue, largely leave mastery (i.e. more than digital competence) of the form to pupils themselves.

However, this is not the case with content. Pupils must learn about digital risks relating to abuse, crime, mistrust, privacy and wellbeing, while also learning about digital opportunities relating to learning, making connections, leisure, employment and citizenship. We can address content through whole-school strategies as well as focused lessons. It is around these digital risks and opportunities that the Futureproof framework is built.

THE THEORY UNDERPINNING THE FRAMEWORK

This is predominantly a practical book that explains how to organise a character-based approach to digital citizenship in schools. It is, however, underpinned by theory. Although many might skim through this section, it is important to understand that the framework we propose is not built on thin air but on thousands of years of thinking about how we might live best in the world.

We have drawn on three moral theories and utilised these in combination. We might call this process pragmatic theorising: utilising, revising and combining established theories to help us tackle an issue. At their simplest, moral theories inform how we might decide to behave in any given situation. Much of the time they operate at a subconscious level – for example, we know when getting in the car how to drive to try to avoid harm to others (i.e. what side to drive on, how to be a courteous driver, what might happen if we go too fast, etc.). Such decisions, if we spend time thinking about them, can be broadly classified against the following three moral theories.

- **Utilitarianism** is based on the principle that the 'right thing to do' is the action that brings the greatest happiness for the greatest number of people, and draws on the philosophy most commonly associated with Jeremy Bentham and John Stuart Mill.

- **Deontology** is based on the moral principle that it is one's duty to follow rules and guidelines, and draws on the philosophy most commonly associated with the philosopher Immanuel Kant. Most schools run on deontological principles: they set rules about behaviour, draw up policies to guide school life and implement codes on staff conduct.

- **Virtue ethics** is a theory that originates in the ancient Greek philosophy of Aristotle. His argument is that if we want to help people to 'do the right thing' then we have to educate them in character and virtue.

Below, we describe how we have brought each of these theories up to date and used their most useful insights to serve our current purpose.

DIGITAL FLOURISHING - UTILITARIANISM

In the most basic terms, utilitarian philosophy relates to making judgements about the best course of action on the basis of calculations. For example, a classic utilitarian dilemma might be: would you save one member of your family from one part of a building on fire if it means that four people you do not know might die in another part of the building? Whether we think about it or not, utilitarian philosophy is behind many of the decisions teachers make in schools. Think about issues such as whether you put more effort into one pupil with special needs over the rest of the class; whether you spend your budget on trips or on wall displays. The answers to these questions will depend on what the school community normatively believes to be most important – the utility value of each option. In our framework we use utilitarian approaches to define what should be the ultimate goal of digital citizenship education.

In the framework, we define its utility or desired goal in terms of digital flourishing. Utility is achieved when our online engagements contribute to a notion of the common good. Digital flourishing should be viewed as a form of authentic happiness, where collective wellbeing and happiness are prized over individual pleasure, hedonism or indulgence. On this reading, digital flourishing requires users of digital technologies to take moral actions that enhance rather than diminish the lives of others, and to strive to avoid committing online harms. This might be viewed as the goal for living in the digital age, or what Kristján Kristjánsson calls 'a general blueprint of the good life' that can be conveyed 'through teaching: a consciously accessible, comprehensive and systematic – if also flexible and open-textured – conception of what makes a human life go well'.[38]

Our framing of digital flourishing as the utility value of our framework has many benefits, but also suffers from some of the standard objections to utilitarianism – namely, that it is difficult to predict the consequences of our and others' actions. It is further limited by the fact that the affordances of digital technologies make online actions hard to predict. For example, many young people are left with problematic digital footprints because of items they have posted or tweeted in the past. Likewise, many young people report that they accidentally bullied someone else, as they were not able to see how their post might be interpreted or where it might end up. The same issue applies to sexting, rife in many schools, as pupils are not always able to predict the consequences of sharing explicit pictures with their boyfriend or girlfriend. This does not render utilitarian approaches useless – it just limits them.

There are two important tasks that utilitarian theory can help with – tasks that contribute to the overall goal of digital flourishing. First, schools should educate their pupils about what authentic happiness and digital flourishing are, to help them construct an ideal blueprint for living in the digital age. This means encouraging pupils to imagine the digital worlds in which they would like to live, work and play. Second, schools can incorporate activities into their curricula that prepare pupils to think about the consequences of their online actions. These activities will likely include stimuli like films and stories that provide insight into others' digitally mediated lives.

The aim of utilitarian-based educational activities would be: to help pupils develop an insight into the potentially traumatic effects of their digital interactions, allowing them to pause and reflect before they act; to get them to consider the potential outcomes of their online actions, from the relatively passive and unthinking unidirectional habits of liking, retweeting and following to the more troubling and deliberately aggressive behaviours, including trolling and cyberbullying. Relatedly, another aim is to encourage empathy and a sense of reciprocity in pupils, in the hope that they become increasingly other-regarding in their digital interactions.

DIGITAL RULES – DEONTOLOGY

Rules-based approaches are commonly used by schools to manage their pupils' access to and use of digital technologies and, as such, are one of the core components of the Futureproof framework.

Until now, governments and other enforcement bodies have found it very difficult to regulate big tech companies. There are cases of countries like China banning some apps, but on the whole companies such as Apple, Facebook and Google operate in ways that are largely un- (or certainly under-) regulated. This is for a number of reasons, including:

- Big tech companies are big beasts with lots of power, which makes regulation difficult.
- They operate across borders, which makes it challenging to implement rules both nationally and transnationally.
- The tech changes fast, which means it is hard for rules to keep up.

This situation seems to be changing slowly. In the UK, the Online Safety Bill, which is due to come into effect in 2022, means social media companies will be regulated through legislation that will force them to reduce online risks to children.[39] Companies will be required to protect users under a duty of care that will be enforced by the UK's independent media regulator, Ofcom. Those that fail to do so might face fines and could ultimately be banned from operating in the UK. This bill is the first real attempt in this country to apply rules to manage tech companies and time will tell if the rules have teeth. Until then, it is largely up to parents and educators to impose rules.

In our framework, digital rules are the policies, guidelines and codes of conduct that schools should put in place to help their pupils use digital technologies in ways that contribute to digital flourishing. Digital rules may be needed for a number of reasons, including limiting pupils' mobile phone use to when it is necessary for the purpose of positive and constructive learning, ensuring that the online content pupils access at school is appropriate, and making explicit expectations of online behaviour. Digital rules should be constructed with an eye to the future and implemented when they contribute to the development of character and digital wisdom. Digital rules should be understood as both limited and limiting – they will likely be abstract, will not attend to the specifics of every situation, and will primarily be concerned with making clear minimum expectations of behaviour.

Despite prevailing policy, digital rules should not include outright bans of mobile phones or other internet-enabled devices. As mobile phones are deemed to be distracting and/or damaging, many schools have taken steps to ban or limit their use.[40] In some countries (such as France, Israel and some Canadian and Australian states), the policy on school-wide bans has been decided by governments. Although bans have been shown to be broadly supported by the general public[41] and deemed necessary by teachers,[42] if they are enforced too strictly they may hinder the development of digital wisdom. To develop this, pupils have to learn how to live morally well with digital technologies in their lives.

Rules on phone and other technology use are inconsistently implemented by teachers: some ban them in their classrooms completely, while others are more lenient. Furthermore, it has been found that pupils get around rules by using phones in their pockets during the school day,[43] or they use them openly during class.[44] Some teachers resist bans for principled reasons. These include beliefs that it is not helpful to install mindsets in children that phones and technologies are necessarily harmful, and that banning phones diminishes educational opportunities – just think of the recent e-learning revolution largely brought about by the Covid-19 pandemic. For either practical or principled reasons, many teachers do not consider school policies on mobile phone use to be effective.[45] Instead of outright bans, we propose that schools implement a set of ground rules that outline acceptable use, specifying when pupils can use their phones and other digital devices.

Digital rules are conceptualised in our framework as ground rules, as they provide the foundations for character development and growth. They serve to help pupils understand what is expected in terms of appropriate use of digital technologies, and will likely reduce the occurrence of online harms such as cyberbullying on school grounds. Digital rules also ensure that lessons are not inappropriately interrupted when pupils are distracted by looking at their phones. Rules and policies should be commonly agreed among all stakeholders (pupils, parents, teachers) and should be realistic, reasonable and enforceable. The process of constructing them will require the balancing of legal obligations with the realities of student culture and tools. Furthermore, there is no 'off the shelf' blueprint for rules – schools have to construct them based on what works for the communities they serve. School leaders have to rely on their judgement, knowledge and, at times, instinct when constructing bespoke policies on internet access and use.

Guiding the development of digital rules should be two questions:

- How do they contribute to digital flourishing in society?
- How do they contribute to the cultivation of digital wisdom in pupils?

Providing good answers to these questions is essential if the aim of our framework is to be realised. Given the challenges associated with enforcing rules in the digital world, pupils are as likely to follow them due to the character qualities they possess as they are to follow them simply because they exist. There might be times when pupils make a character-based decision to break a rule for a moral reason. For example, pupils should be able to use their mobile phones to call for assistance in an emergency. Less dramatically, pupils might access their phones during a lesson to help them complete a learning task. Pupils with digital wisdom will know when rules are to be followed and when it is necessary to break them for a greater moral purpose.

DIGITAL CHARACTER – VIRTUE ETHICS

Character is central to our framework as, ultimately, pupils have to learn to manage their own use of digital technologies in ways that are guided by virtues. This requires schools to focus on the cultivation of what Shannon Vallor calls 'techno-moral virtues',[46] of which the most important, for us, is digital wisdom.[47] The framework places virtue ethics at the centre and digital wisdom as the core component around which schools should build their strategies. This is because the overall aim of the framework is to inculcate virtues and digital wisdom in pupils, so they can autonomously manage their use of digital technologies in a way that contributes to their own and others' happiness, wellbeing and overall flourishing. The requirement is for schools to take a planned, conscious and reflective approach to developing character qualities, through being explicit about their character education offering.

Character education, inspired by virtue ethical philosophy, has been experiencing a resurgence in schools in many countries. This has been driven by an understanding that overly narrow curricula, with an exclusive focus on knowledge and attainment, are not sufficient to help children respond to the demands of the day and the future. For example, the Organisation for Economic Co-operation and Development (OECD) has actively explored how to introduce a new set of Programme for International Student Assessment (PISA) tests that measure character and social-emotional outcomes alongside the current tests of maths and science.[48] Such a move has been replicated by some countries. Singapore has placed character and citizenship at the heart of its educational offer, and in the UK the national inspection body, Ofsted, has defined character as one of the outcome measures in its new framework. As these countries and others develop strategies, approaches and curricula for character education, it is incumbent on them to ensure a focus on living well in the digital age.

The term 'character education' has been variously defined and applied. In this book, we advocate that character education must be underpinned by virtue ethical moral theory, as it is the theory most suitably attuned to meet the moral demands posed by digital technologies. When it is underpinned by virtue ethics, character education is less likely to be challenged on grounds that it is indoctrinating, paternalistic and conservative,[49] despite also retaining a primary focus on moral and intellectual virtues. We do not have space to expand on these critiques in this book, but wish to make the case that virtue ethics is well placed to defend character education from these critiques as it respects individual autonomy and difference (see the Jubilee Centre for Character and Virtues' framework for character education in schools[50] for a fuller exploration of this argument).

What is key is that virtue-based character education does not focus on blindly instructing children in how to behave well online, but seeks to cultivate and hone digital wisdom. Digital wisdom can be defined as a meta virtue that enables us to do the right thing, at the right time, in the right way, when using digital technologies. It is a multi-component construct, an intellectual virtue and, importantly, a paradigmatically human quality honed over time through experimentation and critical reflection on action. We develop the quality through our experiences of living in the digital world, and by sometimes making mistakes and learning from them.

In this book, we complement some of our other publications by outlining what an explicit approach to character education for digital flourishing might look like. We go into more depth in part 2. For now, it suffices to know that key elements of the approach include: providing pupils with a language of character and an understanding of why different virtues – including honesty, compassion, justice, courage and wisdom – matter in day-to-day digital interactions; and utilising this language to help pupils reflect on their day-to-day experiences of living in the digital age and the decisions they make – a form of experiential learning.

A reconstructed character education-based approach, as advocated in this book, might look as follows. First, pupils are judged not on whether they comply with a set of rules, but on the character qualities they display in their day-to-day digital interactions. Second, education starts with pupils' experiences of using digital technologies, not with worksheets about abstract examples or principles. Third, children are taught a language of character that frames their evaluation of their digital interactions; they learn to ask, is this the compassionate, honest or just action to take? Fourth, the approach allows children to make mistakes, and support and mentoring is provided to help them learn from their mistakes. Fifth, the focus is on honing the overarching quality of digital wisdom (putting the virtues into practice in real life), not just on the individual virtues themselves.

Such a virtue-led approach can be bolstered by drawing on deontological and utilitarian approaches. There will be times when it is necessary to remove phones as well as implement codes of conduct that outline acceptable use. Likewise, it is useful to share examples with pupils of the consequences of online actions that have resulted in online harm, such as children who have killed themselves after being bullied. These experiences can build the moral consciousness of pupils and inform their thinking when they try to calculate the consequences of their own actions.

Having presented the moral theories central to our framework, we will now turn to the important task of showing how these are integrated to inform a new approach to practice.

INTRODUCING THE FRAMEWORK: CORE COMPONENTS AND OBJECTIVES

In this section, we provide a big-picture overview of the three core components in our framework and its six interrelated objectives (two per component). We go into much greater detail about each of these in part 2 and show how they can be implemented in practice using examples.

Drawing on the moral theories we have outlined, the three core components of the framework and its interrelated objectives are as follows.

COMPONENT 1: DIGITAL FLOURISHING

Digital flourishing is defined as the ability to live well in a digital world worth living in. This is the overall objective of the framework. All decisions, ranging from how to develop digital citizenship curricula to how pupils should behave when using technologies, should be aimed towards digital flourishing. As such, our definition of this term is informed by a value-rich understanding of utilitarian philosophy, whereby decisions and actions are directed towards this goal – digital flourishing is the utility value.

In order for pupils to understand what digital flourishing is and why it is important in their and others' lives, schools must fulfil the following two objectives.

- **Objective 1: digital vision**. Pupils need to share a vision for digital flourishing that they can employ to evaluate how they use digital technologies and their digital interactions. This means they need to be able to construct, together, imaginaries of what the digital world should look like for it to be worth living in.

- **Objective 2: digital literacy.** Pupils need to share a common language and a set of functional and critical skills and knowledge about digital technologies – from practical, operational skills to the ability to critically evaluate online content and the broader digital environment.[51] Digital literacy is traditionally understood as an integral part of digital citizenship.[52] What is unique about our approach is that it is understood here as a set of skills and knowledge that need to be deployed in ways that contribute to digital flourishing.

COMPONENT 2: DIGITAL RULES

Digital rules are the principles, rules and guidelines that inform behaviour and actions to ensure that these contribute to digital flourishing. They should outline a set of minimum expectations of pupils' behaviour in terms of how they use digital technologies.

The digital rules that schools need to put in place should be evident in the following ways.

- **Objective 3: digital policies.** Pupils need to adhere to a commonly shaped and agreed set of policies about when digital technologies can be used and for what purpose. This includes policies on whether and to what extent digital devices may be used in the classroom and on school grounds.

- **Objective 4: netiquette.** Pupils need to create and adhere to a set of guidelines that ensure they use digital technologies in ways that contribute to human flourishing. This includes guidelines for what may be considered appropriate or not in terms of pupils' online behaviour.

COMPONENT 3: DIGITAL CHARACTER

Digital character refers to the human qualities that pupils and staff need to develop if they are to use digital technologies in a way that minimises digital risks and maximises digital opportunities. Pupils who act with character will have elevated expectations for how they and others should interact when using digital technologies. The building blocks of character are virtues, the most important of which is digital wisdom.

In order to support pupils to develop digital character, schools must fulfil the following two objectives.

- **Objective 5: digital virtues**. Pupils need to possess and be able to deploy character qualities (e.g. compassion, honesty, integrity, resilience) that can help them and others to digitally flourish.

- **Objective 6: digital wisdom**. Pupils need to possess wisdom that enables them to act with deliberation and discernment in relation to how they use digital technologies. They need to be able to deploy digital wisdom in the context of their digital interactions and in ways that can help them to do the right thing at the right time when using these technologies.

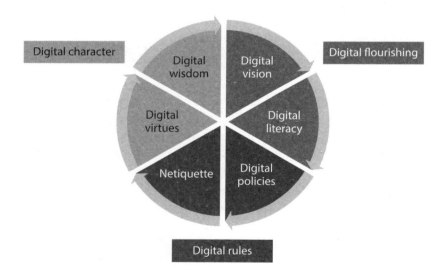

PART 2

THE FRAMEWORK FOR DIGITAL CITIZENSHIP EDUCATION

INTRODUCTION

In this part of the book, we provide more details about our framework for digital citizenship education and show educators how they can put it into practice. This part is divided into three sections covering each of the three core components (and their associated objectives). Initially, we provide a description of each of the components and objectives; then we suggest some examples of how the objectives might be achieved in practice in primary and secondary schools. These examples include strategies, activities and lessons relating to the following aspects of a school.

- **Culture**: how schools might be set up to prioritise a comprehensive approach to digital citizenship education.
- **Curriculum**: the lessons and activities that should be taught about digital citizenship education.
- **Community**: how to work with individuals and organisations in the community (parents, charities, businesses, etc.) to enhance digital citizenship education.

Although the framework provides a clear set of markers to help schools implement a comprehensive approach to digital citizenship education, it is important to remember that schools serve different communities and work in different contexts. Therefore, we believe it is up to school leaders and staff to decide, after some trial and error, which activities work best. The examples we provide will likely need to be adapted to suit local contexts and complemented with additional activities.

THE THREE COMPONENTS AND SIX OBJECTIVES OF THE FUTUREPROOF FRAMEWORK

Component 1: Digital flourishing – *establishing common expectations*

- Objective 1: Cultivate a common digital vision.
- Objective 2: Develop a shared digital literacy.

Component 2: Digital rules – *enforcing minimum expectations*

- Objective 3: Implement commonly agreed digital policies.
- Objective 4: Co-develop and uphold guidance on netiquette.

Component 3: Digital character – *enabling elevated expectations*

- Objective 5: Cultivate digital virtues.
- Objective 6: Nurture digital wisdom.

COMPONENT 1: DIGITAL FLOURISHING – ESTABLISHING COMMON EXPECTATIONS

To flourish online is to live well in a digital world worth living in – this should be the goal at which all digital citizenship activities, strategies and lessons are aimed.

Schools should construct their own visions for digital flourishing, in the same way they construct their own mission statements and core values. Their visions should translate as statements on their common expectations for how digital technologies should be used to contribute to human flourishing. These common expectations for how to live well in the digital age will hopefully be shared by staff, pupils and parents. Relatedly, they will help teachers to decide what policies may be developed and provide some parameters for expected staff and pupil behaviour. Pupils and staff must develop digital literacy that enables them to use digital technologies in line with their understanding of what digital flourishing means in relation to their own lives.

Schools will know they have fulfilled their vision for digital flourishing when:

- Pupils feel they are healthy, happy and living well in the digital world.
- Pupils are contributing to their own and others' health, happiness and ability to live well in the digital world.

Digital flourishing is about individual pupils and broader society. It is when pupils take actions that ensure their own happiness and wellbeing, and balance these against actions that ensure those around them are also happy and well. In short, it is about individual pupils and their communities flourishing together in the digital age.

Of course, many aspects that contribute to digital flourishing are beyond schools' control. Digital flourishing on a societal and even an individual scale depends on factors such as quality parenting, how tech is developed, government policies, pupils' character and many more. Schools should ensure that pupils understand the importance of digital flourishing and how they can contribute to it. Learning and personal development undertaken in schools will influence how pupils behave both within and outside the school gates – and, importantly, in the future.

FIVE DOMAINS OF DIGITAL FLOURISHING

The Human Flourishing Program at Harvard University suggests six domains of human life that individuals can use to measure whether they are flourishing.[53] We have adapted this measure in order to provide a simple way for pupils to think about how – and to assess whether they believe – they are flourishing in the digital age. Although the measure will only give a general, largely subjective, flourishing 'score', it can be a useful way to get pupils to think about the domains of digital flourishing and evaluate whether they are scoring higher in some than others.

The adapted measure consists of two questions for each of the five relevant domains (we have omitted the sixth domain, 'financial and material stability', as this is of less relevance to our current purposes). Each of the questions can be assessed on a scale of 0-10. The digital flourishing score can be obtained by adding together the scores from each of the 10 questions, resulting in a total score from 0 to 100.[54]

NB: The term 'digital technologies' refers to smartphones, laptops, computers, tablets, gaming machines, etc.

Domain 1: happiness and life satisfaction

1. Do you think digital technologies contribute to your happiness and life satisfaction?

0 = not at all, 10 = completely

2. In general, how happy or unhappy do you usually feel when using digital technologies?

0 = extremely unhappy, 10 = extremely happy

Domain 2: mental and physical health

3. In general, do you think digital technologies have a positive or negative effect on your physical health?

0 = negative, 10 = positive

4. In general, do you think digital technologies have a positive or negative effect on your mental health?

0 = negative, 10 = positive

Domain 3: meaning and purpose

5. Overall, to what extent do you feel the things you do using digital technologies are worthwhile?

0 = not at all worthwhile, 10 = completely worthwhile

6. I understand my purpose for using digital technologies in my life.

0 = strongly disagree, 10 = strongly agree

Domain 4: character and virtue

7. I always act to promote good in all circumstances when using digital technologies, even in difficult and challenging situations.

0 = not true of me, 10 = completely true of me

8. I am always able to give up some happiness when using digital technologies now for greater happiness later.

0 = not true of me, 10 = completely true of me

Domain 5: close social relationships

9. I am happy about the friendships and relationships I make and sustain partially through digital technologies.

0 = strongly disagree, 10 = strongly agree

10. My relationships that are partly mediated through digital technologies are as satisfying as I would want them to be.

0 = strongly disagree, 10 = strongly agree

For more information about Harvard's Human Flourishing Program, and to find out more about the six domains and the original measure, visit: hfh.fas.harvard.edu

OBJECTIVE 1: CULTIVATE A COMMON DIGITAL VISION
Pupils need a common vision for digital flourishing with which they can evaluate their use of digital technologies and their digital interactions.

Schools need to develop a digital vision that all members of the school community subscribe and aspire to. This digital vision, which might be constructed as a statement, should describe what digital flourishing is and why achieving it should be a common goal that everyone works towards. The vision should also be a public statement about the aims and expected outcomes of the school's approach to digital citizenship education. With technology developing at exponential rates, it is easy to be swayed when writing the vision statement into covering the issues of the day. But the vision should be overarching, encompassing a full range of current and anticipated digital risks and opportunities.

A school's vision for digital flourishing needs to be compelling. It should encourage anyone who uses digital technologies in the school community to buy into it. A clear vision statement ensures that any lessons, assemblies, drop-down days or community activities on digital citizenship are not ad hoc, but are a planned part of the overarching vision and directed at a clearly articulated overall goal. This should help to ensure that digital citizenship education activities are not thought up on the spot, randomly, without planning or reflection. Before any activity is developed and implemented, it is important to ask how it contributes to the overall vision.

Although we say that schools should construct their own vision for digital flourishing, we do provide some pointers here about what the vision might include. Importantly, the state of flourishing should be seen as complete, in terms of human wellbeing.[55] It is important to stress that the focus should be on long-term, authentic flourishing, not on actions that result in short-term happiness. Of course, being happy in the moment is important, but what really matters is flourishing over the duration of a life and across generations. There are many ways in which pupils can find short-term happiness online – for example, playing computer games or online dating. This type of happiness is more fleeting and temporary. The other type of happiness, the one we think really matters, involves a more long-lasting commitment to a particular purpose or meaningful relationship.

When constructing your school's vision, consider the following:

- How to manage the balance between shorter-term and more immediate happiness and a longer-term sense of fulfilment and purpose.
- How to make the vision aspirational but also achievable – it must speak to pupils and staff and be grounded in their everyday realities.
- The particular digital risks and opportunities your pupils are exposed to. Make these central to the vision by reflecting on how pupils may be encouraged to maximise the opportunities and minimise the risks, and how this could be achieved with the support of different players (e.g. educators, parents, tech companies).
- How multiple voices might be included to construct the vision – pupils, parents, teachers, governors and members of the community.
- How often the vision might need revising, given the pace of technological change.
- Careful choice of language so the vision is understood and owned by all members of the school community, avoiding complexity and enabling accessibility for all.

Once the school's vision for digital flourishing is agreed and has been communicated widely, it should guide pupils' interactions that are mediated by digital technologies. The vision should become an aspiration for the school to strive to live up to, and a measure against which the school can assess the nature and consequences of its pupils' engagement with digital technologies.

The question that pupils should learn to ask is, 'Do my online interactions contribute to or diminish the school's vision for digital flourishing?'

PUTTING THE THEORY INTO PRACTICE: EXAMPLES OF A DIGITAL FLOURISHING VISION STATEMENT

Example 1

Pupils and staff at [insert school name] use digital technologies to enhance their own and others' flourishing. The school community will ensure pupils maximise the opportunities that come from using digital technologies, including for learning, promoting citizenship, building meaningful relationships and enhancing employment opportunities. We aim to provide every possible opportunity for our pupils to excel in the use of technology. We recognise that digital technologies allow us to achieve success in a multitude of different ways and that if we empower our pupils with the skills and understanding required to harness the power of technology, they will be better equipped to live in an increasingly digital world.

Meanwhile, as a community we will seek to minimise the risks associated with digital technologies – for example, in terms of citizenship, abuse, safety, mistrust and wellbeing. We will do so in a way that promotes digital literacy skills and knowledge as well as character and wisdom, so that pupils and staff are empowered to use digital technologies independently in a way that improves their own and others' lives. The promotion of digital flourishing will be prioritised in the school ethos and culture, through lessons across the curriculum and in activities that involve parents and the whole community. It is our aim to contribute to the development of digital citizenship among all pupils.

Example 2

We strive to provide all our pupils with the essential skills, knowledge and character virtues to allow them to navigate the ever-changing digital landscape. We educate pupils so they are fully aware of the risks involved with the digital world, which is crucial to keeping themselves safe and protected. However, and equally as important, we inspire pupils to take advantage of the wealth of the opportunities that the digital world brings to them, their learning, their future career and employment prospects, and their relationships. We endeavour to nurture pupils' character to ensure they can make the right decisions, at the right time, for the right reasons, while embracing the power of the digital world and connecting with each other virtually.

We carefully nurture pupils in their journey towards flourishing, and becoming digitally competent and wise adults, through a multifaceted approach. Pupils acquire the essential skills and knowledge they need through the enactment of our personal development curriculum, computing lessons, PSHE lessons, assemblies, form tutor time, and through encounters with employers.

We ensure that our staff are confident and receive the required professional development they need to deliver on this vital part of the curriculum. This progressive approach, throughout the five years that pupils spend in our care, is what helps to develop the goal of digital citizenship. It is this that guides pupils in their online behaviour and activity way beyond the school gates and in line with behaviour policy, and helps to set their virtual moral compass as they transition into adulthood, so they can flourish in their future lives.

PUTTING THE THEORY INTO PRACTICE: CONSULTING ON THE VISION FOR DIGITAL FLOURISHING

The first step in developing a vision for digital flourishing is to gain an understanding of the digital challenges and opportunities relevant to the school's context. This will ensure the vision is a good fit for the needs of the pupils and the school community. It is also enlightening to find out the real issues perceived by the school community; these can shape the direction of not only the vision itself but also the school improvement plan, curriculum design and so on.

Gaining rich evidence from teachers, parents and pupils can aid the construction of the vision, taking into account that the issues experienced by parents within the household in relation to their children's use of digital technologies (which are likely to be dependent on the level of resources readily available within the home) could differ vastly from those encountered within school settings. The use of these technologies may be beneficial for capturing this type of evidence, which could be gathered, for example, by using online forms to survey the opinions of parents and their children. In addition, sessions could be organised to capture the opinions of pupils themselves in relation to the risks and opportunities presented by digital technologies. Sessions run by peers may be highly informative while allowing a more organic and natural conversation to flow. Indeed, it is only from speaking to pupils that educators can gain such valuable insights into how digital technologies are used. These sessions should be a regular part of the school development plan.

Pupils' voices should also be heard in the process of ensuring that a school's digital vision and actions remain absolutely responsive to the children that the school serves. The vision and policies that the school implements may be revised during the academic year depending on the issues encountered by pupils at a given point in time. The digital world progresses at pace, so it is imperative to constantly review and gather new evidence. Each year, a plethora of new platforms and applications are released that allow pupils to connect and communicate freely. There is usually a time lag before teachers catch up with the new technologies and any issues that pupils might experience as a result of using these technologies. This is why cultivating digital citizenship is so important, as is developing a shared digital vision in collaboration with pupils and the wider community.

Alongside informal discussion with pupils, asking them to draft, together with school staff, versions of their school's vision statement can be a great exercise – one that should be implemented in ways that are mindful of pupils' ages. It might be useful to create a shorter and more accessible version of the statement for primary school children. For example:

> We are committed to equipping our pupils with the necessary skills and knowledge to allow them to make the right decisions when online, empowering them to be responsible digital citizens of the future.

It is important that the vision statement is written with an awareness of how it fits with the existing mission statement/s of the school, in order to ensure coherence. Sharing the vision with the school community is equally crucial to ensure collective buy-in. This could be achieved via newsletters, the school website, assemblies, open mornings and the posting of videos, which has proven, more recently, to be a helpful method of conveying messages in a quick and easy way. Depending on the school's context and prevalent issues, care may need to be taken to ensure that the vision is accessible for all to understand, particularly pupils who speak English as an additional language.

OBJECTIVE 2: DEVELOP A SHARED DIGITAL LITERACY

Pupils need a common language to talk about digital technologies, as well as functional and critical skills and knowledge – from practical, operational skills to the ability to critically evaluate online content and the broader digital environment in a way that contributes to digital flourishing.

A shared digital literacy is necessary for teachers and pupils alike to understand and strive to fulfil their school's vision for digital flourishing. It will also help them to think autonomously and critically about how to best use technologies in ways that enhance their own and others' lives.

It is important to make a distinction between a narrow and a wider understanding of digital literacy. A narrow definition of digital literacy relates to the skills and knowledge required to use digital technologies practically, which can be understood as functional digital literacy. This type of literacy is important for pupils to learn but is insufficient on its own. Alongside developing functional digital literacy, pupils need **critical digital literacy**. This refers to the skills and knowledge required to critically evaluate online content – for example, in relation to issues of bias and trustworthiness as well as the broader digital environment, from how internet corporations operate to the impact had by digital technologies on individuals and society at large.[56] So, it is essential that pupils learn not just how to practically use digital technologies and how these work, but also what it means to interact with others and participate in society in ways that are mediated by these technologies, and how the technologies contribute to the way people feel, think and act. This requires a language that is wider and less technical; a language that is more philosophical, psychological and sociological. This critical digital literacy would help pupils to answer questions such as:

- Do digital technologies add to or reduce my happiness and wellbeing?
- Are digital technologies making me a better person?
- What do I fear most about living in the digital world?
- How would I describe my relationship with my smartphone?
- Am I in charge of my smartphone or is it in charge of me?
- Are some digital technologies better for me than others?
- How would I like digital technologies to shape the world of the future?
- How can I expect society to change because of digital technologies?
- What are the benefits and limitations of using digital technologies for interacting with others and participating in society as citizens in the digital age?

Topics that might be addressed through the possession of a narrow definition of digital literacy	Topics that might be addressed through the possession of a broader definition of digital literacy
How to use a laptop.	How to critically evaluate information found online.
How to make a PowerPoint presentation.	How digital technologies relate to my own and others' happiness.
How to code.	How digital technologies contribute to but also reduce human flourishing.
How to use video editing software.	How to evaluate the impact of my social media posts.
How to use a search engine.	How data harvesting affects me.
How to programme a computer.	How and when to deploy digital skills and knowledge to demonstrate my digital wisdom.

Primary schools should provide direct support to their pupils to help them develop a basic digital literacy, adding more complex words, ideas and concepts as pupils move through the school. Secondary schools should provide opportunities for pupils to use this language to think critically and reflectively, allowing them to feel comfortable putting the language into everyday use. Both primary and secondary schools need to introduce new terms and concepts related to the digital age as they emerge and become relevant.

PUTTING THE THEORY INTO PRACTICE: DOES THE INTERNET MAKE THE WORLD A BETTER PLACE?

The intention of the following activity is to get pupils to explore a big question: does the internet make the world a better place? Before starting the activity, the teacher should explicitly teach some vocabulary so pupils have a shared understanding and a common language. The vocabulary might include some of the following terms.

- FOMO – fear of missing out.
- Trolling.
- Mental health and wellbeing.
- Connection.
- Catfishing.
- Opportunities.
- Employment.
- Risk.
- Mistrust.
- Privacy.
- Grooming.
- Fraud.
- Digital wisdom.
- Digital footprint.
- Personal brand.

For some of the more complex or abstract vocabulary, such as 'digital wisdom', the teacher may want to explore the etymology and use a graphical breakdown such as a Frayer model to provide greater understanding to pupils. The Frayer model[57] is a technique that can be used to explicitly teach vocabulary to pupils. It is a simple visual model to help students organise their understanding of a new academic term or complex piece of vocabulary.

Teacher-led section

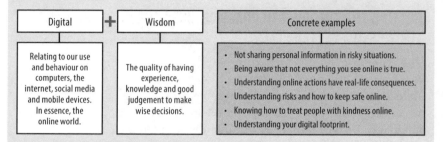

To begin explicitly teaching the term 'digital wisdom', for example, the teacher might create a mind map under a visualiser with 'digital wisdom' in the centre. The teacher may then want to unpack what each word (i.e. 'digital' and 'wisdom') means, asking pupils to contribute and checking for understanding. If a visualiser is not available, the same process could be modelled on a PowerPoint slide that could be left on the screen while pupils complete the independent task to follow. It may be useful for the teacher to share imagery, dual coding, symbols or news items that link to each term used; this is so pupils can process and connect the new information as the mind map builds. Pupils are to build the mind map in their notebooks as the class discussion progresses. The purpose is to build broad foundational knowledge that can be explored in greater depth in subsequent lessons.

Next, present pupils with a moral dilemma, such as the one below, and encourage them to think about how they would approach the situation.

Your best friend has told you in the lunch queue that they have set up a fake alias Instagram account as a joke. They have been targeting a new pupil who started the school a few weeks ago as a mid-term admission. Your friend has been leaving nasty comments on the pupil's feed, such as 'No friends' and 'No one likes you'. Your friend says that they 'spam' this person's Instagram account daily.

The teacher should pose the following questions.

- What action do you take in this situation?
- Is it right to report your friend for online bullying, or do you stay loyal?
- What emotions might the victim be feeling?
- What might be the reasons why your friend is posting these comments?

Independent practice

Pupils could be asked to write an argument in their notebooks to support the big question – does the internet make the world a better place? – and produce a counterargument to challenge it. To scaffold, the teacher may find it useful to provide some pupils with writing prompts:

- I think that...
- In my opinion…
- I would agree with the big question because…
- I would disagree with the big question because…
- Building on what I said previously…
- In conclusion, my view is…

Pupils could be given 30 minutes to complete this section of the activity. The teacher may find it useful to circulate the room, identifying and addressing misconceptions, and asking pupils to verbalise parts of their argument to the class in order to demonstrate/model good practice. This is an excellent opportunity for praise, which can serve as a catalyst for engagement. At the end of the 30 minutes, the teacher could ask pupils to share their ideas and elaborate on points raised in order to facilitate class discussion. The teacher should promote and correct the use of the shared vocabulary introduced at the start of the lesson. As pupils communicate sections of their arguments, the teacher may find it useful to ask the rest of the class to note down any points they have not considered in a different colour pen.

Homework: flipped learning

The teacher may ask pupils to research one real-life example/case study of when a celebrity or sports figure has been trolled, bullied or treated cruelly online. Pupils should be asked to provide the following.

- A brief account of what happened to the celebrity or sports figure. This could include a news article or a written synopsis by the pupil.
- An explanation of the impact the event had on the person's happiness and wellbeing.
- An explanation of the action taken by the person in response to the incident.

PUTTING THE THEORY INTO PRACTICE: DO DIGITAL TECHNOLOGIES ADD TO OR REDUCE MY HAPPINESS AND WELLBEING?

This activity follows on from the previous one. It considers in greater detail some of the risks and opportunities of digital technologies explored in pupils' mind maps and written arguments. Pupils are required to explore another big question: do digital technologies add to or reduce my happiness and wellbeing?

Do It Now activity (retrieval practice)

As pupils enter the classroom at the start of the lesson, the teacher may ask them to explain the following terms (taken from the first activity) without supporting material. This will encourage pupils to think hard and practise retrieving the knowledge from their long-term memories.

- Digital wisdom.
- Wellbeing.
- Privacy.
- Grooming.

After five minutes, the teacher should ask pupils for their responses, correcting and adding detail. This is a good way for the teacher to address any misconceptions at the start of the lesson.

Explicit teaching of new vocabulary

It is important that the teacher once again explicitly and deliberately teaches the key vocabulary in order to foster a shared understanding. The teacher may want to use a simple graphical template after the Do It Now activity – see the example below. Pupils should summarise the vocabulary in their notebooks.

TODAY'S ESSENTIAL VOCABULARY – BUILDING YOUR WORD BANK			
Trolling	**FOMO** FEAR OF MISSING OUT	**'Like' culture**	**Social media addiction**
A person who intentionally tries to instigate conflict, hostility, or arguments online. Trolls often use inflammatory messages to provoke emotional responses out of people.	The fear of missing out is the perception that others are having more fun or living better lives than you are. It affects self-esteem and is often exacerbated by social media.	This is where people become fixated on the number of likes they receive on a picture or post on social media. This can impact on happiness and self-esteem.	Social media addiction is overly using social media: the urge to log in to or use social media and devoting so much time to it that it impairs other important life areas.

Using homework to facilitate class discussion

With a partner, pupils can explain the research they completed for their homework after the first activity (see page 76). Pupils should each spend three minutes verbally summarising their findings, ensuring they cover the three points set out in the homework. After all the pupils have shared their homework, the teacher may find it useful to pick out some examples and ask pupils to share their findings more widely with the class. The teacher could ask some of these probing questions:

- How might the incident have made the celebrity/sports figure feel and why would they feel like that?
- What may have been the motive of the person who targeted the celebrity/sports figure?
- What action would you have taken in this situation?
- What support mechanisms are available if we encounter a situation like this?
- How could we support one of our friends experiencing a situation like this?

Teacher-led case study: Caroline Flack

The teacher may introduce a case study (via a video or article) about the television and radio presenter Caroline Flack. The case study shows how Flack suffered relentless online abuse and was targeted by constant headlines during a troubled time in her life. This impacted so negatively on her mental health that she took her own life.

This case study encourages pupils to critically appreciate some of the limitations that the internet may present for wellbeing, while suggesting that unkindness online may have an impact on people in the offline world. This is why users should show virtues such as kindness, compassion and empathy online.

Independent task

The teacher may ask pupils to use a ruler to divide a page of their notebooks into two. At the top of one column, pupils write the title 'Improves happiness and wellbeing', and on the other 'Reduces happiness and wellbeing'. The teacher asks pupils to write down, and more importantly explain, which aspects of the digital world or technologies add to happiness and wellbeing and which could be considered to reduce happiness and wellbeing. The teacher should give pupils 30 minutes to complete the task. During this time, the teacher may find it useful to circulate the classroom, pick out responses and ask pupils to elaborate/explain so as to check for understanding. After the 30 minutes is over, the teacher may instigate a class discussion on pupils' thoughts on which digital elements add to/detract from happiness and wellbeing. In doing so, the teacher could ask pupils to provide counterarguments to the points that have been raised.

Homework: independent student reflection

Pupils may be asked to reflect in their notebooks on the big question: do digital technologies add to or reduce my happiness and wellbeing? This is to encourage pupils to think about and reflect on their personal use of digital technologies, in order to become more self-aware users of these technologies. It may be helpful to provide pupils with the following questions as prompts.

- How do you feel when your pictures or posts do not get many likes on social media (e.g. Facebook, Instagram)?
- What emotions do you feel when you check your social media?
- How often do you pick up your phone (this is measurable on most mobile devices)? Is this a shock? If so, why?
- Do you edit your pictures before you post them on social media? If so, why?
- How does connecting with friends and family through social media and messaging apps make you feel?

COMPONENT 2: DIGITAL RULES – ENFORCING MINIMUM EXPECTATIONS

Digital rules are the guidelines, policies and expectations that schools must put in place to help pupils interact with digital technologies in a way that contributes to the vision for digital flourishing.

Digital rules enforce the minimum expectations for digital technology use in school. For example, these rules might specify the appropriate times for pupils to use smartphones on school premises (if at all), what content can be accessed, and aspirations for how pupils and staff should interact online. The rules should be developed by senior leaders in consultation with staff, pupils and parents and take into consideration developments in technology. They should be reviewed annually and all staff, parents and pupils should be made aware of them. Although it is important that rules are imposed, mainly to protect pupils, they are insufficient on their own. The decision about whether a rule is required should be made after considering the following questions.

- Is the rule necessary to protect pupils from online risks and keep them safe?
- Is the rule necessary to improve pupil's ability to build the knowledge, skills and character that will help them to flourish in the 21st century?

If the answer to either of these questions is yes, the rule is probably justified. If the answer to both of these questions is no, the rule is probably not necessary – and it might actually hinder pupils' ability to cultivate the character qualities and wisdom required for living in the digital age.

OBJECTIVE 3: IMPLEMENT COMMONLY AGREED DIGITAL POLICIES

Pupils need to adhere to a commonly shaped and agreed set of policies about when digital technologies can be used and for what purpose.

Schools have to establish policies about how digital technologies are used on school grounds. There are no hard and fast rules, nor is there a 'correct' policy. For example, some schools (mainly secondaries) may encourage pupils to use smartphones at times during the school day for positive purposes, such as to improve learning. Others (mainly primaries) may take smartphones from pupils at the school gate and return them at the end of the day. Many schools have rules somewhere in between – for example, allowing pupils to use their smartphones during break times.

There are growing calls to make classrooms 'phone-free sanctuaries' to improve children's mental health. For example, a coalition of prestigious private schools in the UK recently joined forces with academy trusts such as Oasis and Star to lobby for tighter rules on smartphone use in schools post-lockdown. This coalition published a report arguing that 'the nudges and prods of competing apps and messages should be left at the [classroom] door. This way we will give children and young people the space to build those high-quality peer relationships and the ability free from distraction to focus on learning.'[58]

It is important for schools to have policies on digital technologies (such as when and where smartphones may be used) that are commonly agreed, regularly updated and universally enforced. These policies should set the expectations and help to maintain standards. Having a written policy makes the rules explicit to pupils, staff and parents. Policies should be neither draconian, which may make pupils feel fearful about technologies, nor overly liberal to the extent that smartphone use might distract pupils from their lessons or lead to challenging behaviours. Furthermore, policies should be age-related, with pupils in higher years in secondary schools perhaps given more freedom and choice around smartphone use than those in lower years.

School policies should extend beyond pupils' use of smartphones. There might be a need for policies for staff on smartphone use, particularly as staff model certain behaviours that pupils might follow. Policies should also inform how and when other technologies, like laptops and tablets, should be used and for what purposes. Furthermore, schools need policies on what content can be accessed via these technologies. This can be a tricky decision, because restricting some websites could be considered a form of censorship that is not congruent with a liberal education. However, the teacher's role is to protect pupils from extreme viewpoints and those that are deemed not to contribute to flourishing societies. Decisions about what is appropriate content must be made, in a similar vein to choosing what is (and is not) included in the school curriculum.

Schools are increasingly turning to new technologies to enforce rules and policies. For example, some schools in the UK are now following an approach popular in the US based on lockable pouches. Pupils are expected to lock their phones away at the beginning of the day and can only access them after school. Schools that use lockable pouches have seen a reduction in cyberbullying and other issues related to smartphone use on school premises. As reported in an article in *The Times*, a headteacher from a school in Bedfordshire that uses lockable pouches said that he 'didn't want to ban [smartphones] completely or confiscate them. Now [pupils] can come in and put phones in a pouch after switching them off. I was sceptical but it started working straight away. Now the school is a nicer place, it's more friendly, there's better communication.'[59]

Ultimately, it is important that any rules and policies contribute to rather than hinder the cultivation of digital citizenship among pupils, in ways that are mindful of digital risks and opportunities. With this in mind, it may be helpful for schools to use templates, produced by local authorities and other civil society organisations, that can be adapted to their own policies on pupil use of digital technologies and internet safety. Below is a list of a few example templates, provided by:

- **Kelsi**: www.kelsi.org.uk/child-protection-and-safeguarding/e-safety
- **NSPCC Learning**: learning.nspcc.org.uk/research-resources/templates/online-safety-policy-statement-and-agreement
- **Optimus Education**: my.optimus-education.com/school-model-policy-templates-meet-your-legal-requirements#Statutory
- **SWGfL**: www.swgfl.org.uk/resources/online-safety-policy-templates

- **The Education People**: www.theeducationpeople.org/our-expertise/safeguarding/template-policies-and-guidance
- **UK Safer Internet Centre**: www.saferinternet.org.uk/guide-and-resource/teachers-and-school-staff/online-safety-policy

PUTTING THE THEORY INTO PRACTICE: A PUPIL AGREEMENT ON ICT USE IN A PRIMARY SCHOOL

The following example has been adapted from the version used at Seymour Road Academy, part of Wise Owl Trust, Manchester.

Think then click

We use computers, the internet and lots of other new technologies to help us learn. To keep us safe when using them, we must:

- Ask permission before using the internet.
- Only use websites that an adult has chosen.
- Immediately close any website we are unsure about.
- Tell an adult if we see anything we are uncomfortable with.
- Only email and message people an adult has approved.
- Only send emails and messages that are polite and friendly.
- Do not open emails sent by anyone we do not know.
- Never give out personal information or passwords.
- Never arrange to meet anyone we do not know.
- Do not use internet chat rooms or social networking sites.

Pupils' agreement

- I have read and I understand the online safety rules.
- I will use the computer, network, internet access and other new technologies in a responsible way at all times.
- I know that network and internet access can be monitored.
- If I fail to follow these rules then I may not be allowed to use the computer, network, internet or other new technologies in school.

PUTTING THE THEORY INTO PRACTICE: A SAFER INTERNET USE POLICY

The following example is from St Mary's Catholic High School in Wigan, Manchester.

Information for parents

As part of the school's curriculum, we offer pupils supervised access to the internet. Before being allowed to use the internet, all pupils must obtain parental permission, and both they and you must sign and return the enclosed form as evidence of your approval and their acceptance of the school rules on this matter. All access to the internet is controlled by a comprehensive filter, which restricts access to a vast number of websites. While our aim for internet use is to further educational goals and objectives, pupils may find ways to access other materials as well. We believe that the benefits to pupils from access to the internet, in the form of information resources and opportunities for collaboration, exceed any disadvantages.

During school, teachers will guide pupils towards appropriate materials while discussing issues such as internet safety, social media and cyberbullying. The school reserves the right to monitor a student's computer activities, internet and email usage.

The school encourages pupils to use the rich information resources available on the internet, together with the development of appropriate skills to analyse and evaluate such resources. These skills will be fundamental in the society our pupils will be entering.

Online services significantly alter the information landscape for schools by opening classrooms to a broader array of resources. In the past, teaching and library materials could usually be carefully chosen. All such materials would be chosen to be consistent with national policies, supporting and enriching the curriculum while considering the varied teaching needs, abilities and developmental levels of pupils. Internet access will open classrooms to electronic information resources that have not been selected by teachers as appropriate for use by pupils. Electronic information research skills are now fundamental to the preparation of citizens and future employees in the digital age.

Access will be controlled by means of a filtered service that restricts access to undesirable materials. Access to online resources will enable pupils to explore thousands of webpages while exchanging messages with people throughout the world. As mentioned above, the school believes that the benefits to pupils from access to information resources and increased opportunities for collaboration far exceed the disadvantages.

Student guidelines for internet use

Students are responsible for good behaviour on the internet just as they are in a classroom or a school corridor. General school rules apply in the digital world.

The internet is provided for students to conduct research and communicate with others. Parents' permission is required. Remember that internet access is a privilege, not a right, and that access requires responsibility.

Individual users of the internet are responsible for their behaviour and communications online. It is presumed that users will comply with school standards and will honour the agreements they have signed.

Computer storage areas, removable storage and computer usage can be monitored through software installed on the network. Staff may review files and communications to ensure that users are using the system responsibly. Users should not expect that files stored on servers will always be private.

The following are not permitted:

- Sending or displaying offensive messages or pictures.
- Using obscene language.
- Harassing, insulting or attacking others on social media or by email.
- Damaging computers, computer systems or computer networks.
- Installing software.

- Violating copyright laws.
- Using others' passwords.
- Trespassing in others' folders, work or files.
- Intentionally wasting limited resources such as disk space or printer inks.
- Accessing proxy servers.
- Accessing social media.
- Accessing external email accounts.

Notify a member of staff immediately if, by accident, you encounter materials that violate the rules of appropriate use.

Sanctions

- Violations of the above rules will result in a temporary or permanent ban on internet and/or network use.
- Parents will be informed of the nature of the misuse.
- Additional disciplinary action may be added in line with existing practice on inappropriate language or behaviour.
- When applicable, police or local authorities may be involved.

Student internet use agreement

- I will only access the system with my own username and password, which I will keep secret.
- I will not access other people's files or damage their work and data.
- I will only use the internet when I have permission.
- I will use the internet only for activities and work set by school, e.g. homework, class/topic work.
- I will only email people my teacher has approved, and not use the internet for personal or private messages.
- I will not attempt to access social networking sites.
- I will respect the privacy of others. I will not publish their names, addresses, phone numbers or photographs.

- I will not give my home address or telephone number, or arrange to meet someone, unless my parent, carer or teacher has given permission.
- I will not use work from the internet as if it was my own. I will give credit to the sources of materials included in my work.
- I will not try to find or use unacceptable material from the internet.
- I will report any unpleasant material or messages sent to me. I understand that this report would be confidential and would help to protect other students and myself.
- I will not use school resources to subscribe to any goods or services, and will not buy or sell using the internet.
- I will not download software from the internet.
- I will not bring in removable media from outside the school unless I have been given permission.
- I will not send unsuitable emails or messages via social media. The messages I send will be polite, responsible and only signed in my name. This is the same for comments posted on social media platforms.
- I will not attempt to access blocked websites using a proxy site or any other means.
- I will not send anonymous messages.

PUTTING THE THEORY INTO PRACTICE: A ZERO-TOLERANCE POLICY FOR MOBILE DEVICE USE IN SCHOOL

While on the school site, pupils are not allowed to have their mobile phones visible, to ensure that they concentrate entirely on their studies and that, in unstructured time, they are not engaged in activities with a mobile phone that could put themselves or other pupils at risk. Phones must be turned off and stored in school bags throughout the whole school day.

Social media is an increasing issue for all schools. E-safety is very important to us and we would ask that you work with us to keep issues related to social media out of school. Advice on e-safety can be found on our website.

If a student has a mobile phone on school premises, their phone will be confiscated by a member of staff and returned at the end of the school day. All mobile phones remain the responsibility of the child and the school accepts no liability for any mobile phone lost or stolen in school while in the child's possession.

PUTTING THE THEORY INTO PRACTICE: A MORE LIBERAL VIEW ON MOBILE DEVICE USE IN SCHOOL

Provided by Mark Moorhouse, chief executive of Watergrove Trust, Rochdale, Manchester.

In 1999, the National Farmers' Union judged the mobile phone to be the most important invention of the 20th century, and now the vast majority of the children and young people within our care own one. They have the most powerful device for good and ill at their fingertips, with the capacity to make or mar them, and we are considering banning them from schools? How can it be conscionable for us to turn our backs on our moral duty as educators to help our children develop the capacity to regulate, manage and operate ethically in a world where they are so connected yet so unprotected by regulation? They themselves have to learn to control not only the amount of time they use their phones but also the choices they make as consumers and producers of messaging and content. What they habitually consume will mould who they are, ethically and morally. Are we prepared to look away, to keep this complex and critical learning at arm's length, just when children and young people are most impressionable and need us most? And when they are most vulnerable too? When half of children by the age of seven and nearly all children aged 11 possess a device that might enable a stranger to influence, corrupt and exploit them in their own home, feet away from parents and guardians who are none the wiser?

And why? Because having mobile phones in schools is too disruptive and takes up too much time? If you properly risk-assess the potential for immediate deadly harm of a pencil, it would probably prove more dangerous, so should we ban them too? The young people within our care desperately need educators around as they develop the best habits of self-regulated and positive use of their mobile phones. To step away from this obvious iteration of our social responsibility to educate for life would be self-serving at its worst, thinly disguised as a moral hardline. It is nothing of the kind. In fact, it is a dereliction of professional duty when society and the young people within our care need our influence most.

I heard a school leader rail recently that young people can't manage their use of mobile phones. This is not a revelation. Many young people can't yet solve quadratic equations, but the whole point of us being employed by society to run schools is to ensure that the next generation learn what they need to live productively and happily. We are not paid to engage with only the more straightforward and familiar features of this challenge.

Schools have a fundamental role to play in ensuring that the powerful technologies available to pupils enable rather than ruin them. We have the expertise, means and opportunity to achieve this, better than anyone else. It is our job and a matter of professional pride that we do this and do it well.

OBJECTIVE 4: CO-DEVELOP AND UPHOLD GUIDANCE ON NETIQUETTE
Pupils must create and adhere to a set of guidelines that ensure they use digital technologies in ways that contribute to human flourishing.

Netiquette is the popular term used to describe guidelines that establish expected standards of prosocial behaviour online, mainly detailing what is (or is not) considered respectful communication and acceptable behaviour. Netiquette and digital virtues (see Objective 5) are different. Whereas netiquette is normally a set of predetermined general guidelines about behaviour, digital virtues are qualities of character that need to be shown within specific circumstances. So, whereas netiquette guidelines might include things like 'share with discretion' and 'communicate kindly', digital virtues are, for example, 'judgement' and 'compassion'. Netiquette guidelines will make clear to pupils the minimum expectations for their online behaviour. They are also a useful reminder about expected conduct.

There is no official set of netiquette guidelines; schools and organisations are required to compile their own lists. These might include guidelines such as not posting harmful comments, making your identity clear in all communications, respecting privacy, not using offensive language in social media posts, and not sharing sexual images. It is useful for schools to display their netiquette list prominently. However, schools should keep in mind that it is pupils' compliance with these guidelines that ultimately matters, rather than simply the communication of the guidelines.

Teachers should also strive to follow netiquette guidelines, especially if any of their communications on social media platforms are public. Pupils can often track down their teachers' accounts, even if the teacher has used a pseudonym for their Facebook name or Twitter handle. Therefore, schools should do their utmost to minimise the extent to which pupils can access online communication from their own teachers that is not related to their education.

PUTTING THE THEORY INTO PRACTICE: DEVELOPING NETIQUETTE GUIDELINES ALONGSIDE PRIMARY PUPILS

A valuable insight into the kind of netiquette guidelines required within primary schools can be elicited from pupils themselves. In particular, pupils in higher key stages will likely be able to articulate the risks and challenges they encounter online and what actions might be needed to reduce them. Structured conversations with pupils will naturally uncover the ways in which they use their digital devices and therefore the guidelines necessary. The following activity provides an example of how these conversations might be undertaken.

Working in small groups, pupils can think about and share their examples of good manners in the offline world. The teacher may ask pupils to think about how these examples can be reflected online in order to produce class/school guidelines for netiquette. Discussing offline examples in relation to online netiquette will help pupils to overcome the disconnect that some of them experience between their behaviour online and offline.

Asking pupils to share their ideas within the classroom, or maybe even across the school, will encourage them to think more deeply about netiquette guidelines and ensure that these are representative and relevant to all pupils. The school could also organise an assembly in which older pupils discuss their chosen guidelines, including the reasons behind them.

Netiquette guidance should be reviewed regularly in order to identify any need for additional points. For example, the recent increase in the use of online video conferencing may have required new netiquette guidelines, such as keeping cameras on and raising a virtual hand to speak.

Sample netiquette codes developed by primary school pupils

- Be kind. Always remember there is someone at the other end of the message.
- Take time out before replying, remembering to respect yourself and others.
- Remember it is OK to say you don't know, rather than making something up.
- Never give out private information.
- Know how to get help should you need to.
- Ensure that if you have your webcam on, you are properly dressed and aware of your background.
- Do not share photographs of yourself that may be embarrassing.
- Do not pass on embarrassing photographs or messages that may have been shared with you.
- Only add friends that you know.

Netiquette guidelines for an online classroom

- Ensure you have the equipment that may be necessary for the session. For example, pen and paper.

- Ensure you are fully and appropriately dressed.
- Join remote sessions from quiet and calm spaces, not a bedroom.
- Raise a digital hand should you wish to speak and avoid speaking over other participants.
- Remember that everyone is there to learn and has the right to learn.

PUTTING THE THEORY INTO PRACTICE: IMPLICIT AND EXPLICIT WAYS TO HELP PRIMARY PUPILS ADHERE TO NETIQUETTE GUIDELINES

Putting netiquette guidelines to the test in the classroom is a good way to help pupils uphold and further develop them. Role-modelling and allowing pupils to experiment, possibly even making mistakes within the safety of the classroom, are both important parts of the process. Schools in the UK have already seen a shift of focus from the Department for Education that enables schools to sanction poor behaviour choices outside the school gates, including, more recently, online behaviour. Allowing pupils the opportunity to experiment online within the safety of the school will help them to habitualise their behaviour for the good of themselves and others.

Teachers should seek to implicitly and explicitly 'teach' netiquette guidelines across the different age groups, with the intention that online behaviour aligns with offline expectations about appropriate and inappropriate behaviour. Here are some suggestions for how to do this.

- From their early years, children naturally learn what is appropriate behaviour and that there are often consequences for poor choices. We need pupils to also understand what appropriate behaviour is in the digital world, especially when no one is watching. Schools can help pupils by bringing to their attention examples of good and not-so-good decisions about how to behave. With young children, teachers could ask questions such as, 'If someone was mean to you, what would you do?' Teachers may use pupils' answers to inform group discussion. They may ask pupils to think about their responses to the same question with their eyes closed, mimicking what it is like when pupils are online and cannot see other users. Finally, teachers could ask how pupils feel when someone is unkind to them, and how it makes them feel when they are unkind to others.

- Behaviour policies in schools often focus on the building of relationships in order to create harmonious environments for all. It is important for pupils to recognise that this needs to be replicated online, understanding that there is another person at the other end of the message/post/status update, etc. To demonstrate this to pupils, they could send a message to another pupil, either physically or via technology, while blindfolded or in another room. Once the children have received their messages, they could come back together to talk about the differences between communicating face to face and when you can't see the other person.

- The lack of social cues available when reading a message or an online post could lead to a lesson on how the use of language is important. A range of examples could be shared to show how easily words can be misinterpreted. It may be worth explicitly pointing out that it is more difficult to see offence has been caused and to rectify the situation when communication occurs online rather than face to face. Such misunderstandings can sometimes be a catalyst for disagreement.

- Within school, the use of technology could be embraced and children empowered through the sharing of school social media accounts with pupils. For example, in key stage 2 classes, pupils could support staff in writing tweets and seeing them go live. They could also respond to others' tweets in order to practise and showcase good communication. Likewise, negative comments could be discussed with the pupils, asking them to connect different types of online behaviour with real-life events and the feelings of others.

PUTTING THE THEORY INTO PRACTICE: NETIQUETTE GUIDELINES IN SECONDARY SCHOOLS

It is vitally important to set minimum expectations for digital behaviour among secondary pupils, owing to the increased use of digital technologies among this age group. Teachers must provide pupils with netiquette guidance that can help to steer their use of technology in positive ways. From a very pragmatic perspective, teachers must ensure that pupils are aware of the clear redlines and non-negotiables when it comes to using digital technologies like the internet, to ensure they stay safe and protected.

It is not uncommon for schools to display beautifully designed netiquette guidance. However, this does not necessarily mean that pupils will absorb the guidelines and put them into action. Educators therefore need to provide opportunities for netiquette guidelines to be taught and revisited. It is not enough to display these on the school website or behind reception at school; this is merely a tokenistic gesture that will have little impact without further activities that focus on netiquette. Schools and teachers should view the process of developing pupils' positive online behaviour as a form of curriculum in its own right. Unpacking netiquette guidelines and modelling these with pertinent offline examples would be a more effective approach to take.

Generating and launching netiquette guidelines

It is important that the school community has collective ownership of the netiquette guidance that all stakeholders are expected to adopt and abide by. For this to happen, schools must involve the whole community in the formation of guidelines from the start. The opinions of pupils, parents and school staff could be collected via an online survey that asks what the guidance should include. Communication is key from the start, as is taking a democratic leadership approach.

The survey could look something like this:

We are looking to launch/refine our netiquette guidance so that we can support our pupils in behaving positively online and so they remain safe. The digital world is ever-changing, so we want to reach out to our community to ensure that our guidance supports the needs of the children we serve.

- *What examples of positive behaviour do you witness online?*
- *What examples of negative behaviour do you witness online?*
- *What ground rules do you think are important to teach children about using the internet or social media platforms?*

From these three simple questions, schools will be able to collect evidence about their community and use it as a starting point when creating their netiquette guidance. At this point in the design phase, it would be useful to share the evidence gathered with a pupil leadership team (prefects, pupil leaders, pupil council) and collaborate with them to draw up the school's netiquette guidelines. Pupils' input here is invaluable and will contribute to the implementation phase of the guidelines.

Communicating netiquette guidelines to the community is key

This could be achieved via:

- Formal letters to parents and updates on the school website.
- Student leaders presenting the netiquette guidelines to pupils through assemblies. This approach shows that the guidance has been produced in collaboration with pupils.
- Explicitly teaching the guidance with modelled examples through personal development/PSHE lessons or form time. These lessons need to be sequenced and revisited.
- Displaying the guidelines around the school in high-traffic areas.
- Revisiting the guidelines frequently in assemblies.

Sample netiquette guidelines from Childnet International[60]

- **Be respectful.** Everyone has different feelings and opinions, and it is important to respect this online. You may wish to comment on something someone has shared but always remember that behind every account is a real person. If you would not say it to someone's face, the internet is not the place to say it either.

- **Be aware of how your comments might be read**. Strong language, capital letters and exclamation marks can be easily misinterpreted online. In the offline world we have the addition of body language, tone of voice and facial expressions to help us understand what someone has said. We also have the opportunity to rephrase what we say if we are misunderstood in the offline world. When you are online, these are missing. Think – if you were to receive this comment, how would you have felt?

- **Be careful with humour and sarcasm**. It is always great to share jokes with others and it is important to be yourself online and let your personality shine through. However, not everything is always clear online and sometimes people might not realise you are joking. Often people rely on emojis, or text speak, e.g. 'lol', to help show they are not being serious, but it is not guaranteed other people will understand this. Reread what you have written and think – will everyone get the joke?

- **Think about who can see what you have shared**. Privacy settings are a simple way to restrict who can see what you are sharing, but even with these in place nothing is ever truly private online. Make sure you keep as much of your personal information off the internet as possible and never share anything inappropriate or that may get you into trouble. Remember you are only as private as your much public friend.

- **Remember to check friend requests and group invites before accepting them**. The internet is a great place to share content and chat to friends but remember to review any new requests before accepting them. Check if they are from someone you know or were expecting to receive a request from. If a new request is not from someone you know or recognise then it is OK to decline the request.

- **Be forgiving**. The online world can be very different from the offline world so try to be understanding of others when they struggle with online communication. If you see something online that you do not think is appropriate, you can use reporting tools to flag it to the site's safety team. Remember that not everyone will know these rules before posting or realise that they have upset someone else.

PUTTING THE THEORY INTO PRACTICE: WHAT DOES POSITIVE BEHAVIOUR LOOK LIKE ONLINE?

This activity helps to explicitly teach netiquette guidelines to secondary pupils through another big question: what does positive behaviour look like online? The activity can be used to explore and unpack the guidance with pupils and provide some concrete examples against each guideline.

Do It Now activity (retrieval practice)

As pupils enter the classroom at the start of the lesson, the teacher asks them to answer the following questions without any supporting material. This will encourage pupils to think hard and practise retrieving the knowledge from their long-term memories.

- Should our online behaviour be any different to how we behave in the offline world?
- Why is it important to behave in a positive way online?
- What are the consequences if we behave poorly online?

After five minutes, the teacher should ask pupils for their responses, correcting and adding detail. This is a good way for the teacher to address any misconceptions at the start of the lesson.

Explicit teaching of new vocabulary

It is important that the teacher once again explicitly and deliberately teaches the key vocabulary in order to foster a shared understanding.

Main task: unpacking netiquette guidelines

The teacher can share the collaboratively produced netiquette guidance as well as concrete examples of each point. This will allow pupils to further understand the meaning of the guidance and will contribute to its implementation. So, for example, consider this point from the Childnet International guidelines:

- **Think about who can see what you have shared**. Privacy settings are a simple way to restrict who can see what you are sharing, but even with these in place nothing is ever truly private online. Make sure you keep as much of your personal information off the internet as possible and never share anything inappropriate or that may get you into trouble. Remember you are only as private as your much public friend.

The teacher may now share a concrete example of how an inappropriate comment has led to someone getting into trouble. Consider the following example:

> *The UK pop star James Arthur had to cancel his engagements in November 2013 after a Twitter meltdown. The singer used abusive language to One Direction's Louis Tomlinson and X Factor winner Matt Cardle. James unveiled a rap song in which he used a homophobic slur against another musician and told him to shoot himself. He was then officially dropped from Simon Cowell's record label.*

Key questions to explore in class discussion

- Why did James Arthur's record label drop him?
- How might the LGBTQ+ community have felt about his comments?
- Do online actions and comments have consequences?

The teacher could unpack each of the other netiquette guidelines, connecting these with offline examples, over a sequence of lessons. Class discussion may be held around each example. It is important to allow pupils to reflect on the online behaviour witnessed in the examples and explain why it is inappropriate.

COMPONENT 3: DIGITAL CHARACTER – ENABLING ELEVATED EXPECTATIONS

Schools must develop not just competencies in pupils, but also character that will enable them to flourish in the digital age.

This means cultivating character qualities that will help pupils to flourish at school and, more importantly, when they leave school. While rules inform short-term behaviour, character is what matters for longer-term conduct – it is what makes us *us*. It is for this reason that many curriculum resources and educational programmes designed to enhance digital citizenship implicitly focus on human qualities such as compassion, resilience and honesty. However, an explicit and overarching focus on character is often missing.

We believe character should be at the heart of any school's vision for digital citizenship education and this should be reinforced through policies, communications and, most importantly, practice. Character education that takes into account the digital age should be 'taught' in the classroom, present across the school culture and undertaken alongside the school community.

Although much has been written in recent years about character, there has been less of a focus on what might be called 'digital character'. In effect, digital and non-digital character are the same: who we are when online, using smartphones and other technologies, should be the same as who we are when speaking to people at work, at home or on the street. However, we make particular reference to 'digital character' to show that there are certain affordances of the digital age (discussed in part 1; see page 30) that require us to think differently about how we educate pupils. Our use of the term 'digital character' in Component 3 draws attention to how technologies have impacted the way that pupils enact different virtues.

Digital virtues are the qualities pupils must develop if they are to use digital technologies in a way that enables them to avoid or cope with digital risks and pursue digital opportunities. Pupils who act with character will have elevated expectations for how they and others should interact when using their smartphones, laptops, gaming machines and other digital devices. The building blocks of character are the virtues (e.g. compassion, honesty, integrity, resilience), the most important of which is digital wisdom. Schools should provide pupils with activities that help them to develop positive personal strengths, enabling them to use digital technologies wisely and ultimately without supervision.

OBJECTIVE 5: CULTIVATE DIGITAL VIRTUES
Pupils must possess and deploy character qualities that can help them and others to digitally flourish.

Whereas the term 'netiquette' outlines the minimum expectations of behaviour when using digital technologies, digital virtues are more aspirational. They relate to the possession and deployment of key human qualities that contribute to individual and societal flourishing when using digital technologies. There are many virtues that are important in this regard, including honesty, compassion, courage, justice, good judgement and resilience. The important thing is that schools do not just teach pupils what these virtues are, but also encourage them to display them in their day-to-day lives, both offline and online. This does not mean that pupils will always show digital virtues as appropriate – and when they do not, this should be seen as a learning opportunity. Digital virtues are developed through learning, experience and reflection.

It is worth noting, briefly, that some people do not like or use the term 'virtue'. We use it in this book because, as explained in part 1, the digital character component of our framework is informed by the ancient moral theory of virtue ethics. It is, we acknowledge, a term that has gone somewhat out of fashion, but it seems to be becoming more popular again in everyday discourse. Virtues, for us, are modern-day human qualities that all of us must develop if we are to get on with each other and thrive individually and collectively. If educators prefer not to use the term 'virtue' then it can be substituted with other terms such as 'human qualities', 'strengths', 'dispositions' or 'traits'.

Schools may find it helpful to think that digital virtues can be 'caught, taught and sought'. They can be 'caught' through the ethos and culture of the school (and other environments in which pupils grow up). This is why promoting a digital vision is so important, as is encouraging pupils and staff to embody digital virtues. They can be 'taught' insofar as they can be cultivated in pupils through discreet or cross-curricular learning activities. For example, students can learn about digital virtues through reading in English, role play in drama, lessons on democracy in citizenship, and lessons on wellbeing in PSHE. Ultimately, digital virtues need to be 'sought' – we want pupils to seek out times to show, for example, courage, compassion and honesty, especially when no one is watching.

PUTTING THE THEORY INTO PRACTICE: THINKING ABOUT HONESTY ONLINE

Honesty is an important virtue in the offline world, but it is also central to some of the more troubling online concerns, such as misinformation and crime. In this activity (for older KS2 or secondary school children), pupils will discover the importance of honesty online and consider how they display this quality in their own lives. The aim is to ensure that pupils choose honesty when offered the anonymity of the World Wide Web.

The learning intentions are:

- To understand the impact of honesty and dishonesty on oneself and others.
- To understand how to encourage honesty in others by not manipulating the truth.
- To recognise that others may not show honesty online and how to identify this.

- To recognise that the same principles apply to online relationships as to face-to-face relationships, including respect for others even when we are anonymous.

Dilemma 1

The teacher can present the following dilemma to pupils.

In a maths lesson, Millie is struggling to grasp a method. It seems to her that all the other pupils in her class understand what they are doing. When the teacher asks the class if everyone understands what they are doing, Millie joins in with her classmates and says yes, even though she is confused.

This example has been chosen to try to overcome the potential disconnect between online behaviours and offline behaviours. An online example could also be used, or used as a follow-up dilemma.

Class discussion points

- Why do you think Millie nodded with the rest of her class even though she did not understand what she was doing?
- How do you think Millie was feeling?
- What could Millie do differently next time?
- What advice would you give to Millie?

In this situation, an element of peer pressure and wanting to conform can impact on our decision-making when online. The element of peer pressure could be further discussed. For example:

- Have you ever been untruthful because you have followed your friends in their response?
- How does this dishonesty play out online?
- What examples can you give of when someone has been dishonest online?

Dilemma 2

You see a nasty comment online and a lot of your friends are liking it. What do you do?

The teacher could try to learn from pupils whether or not they are influenced by their friends when deciding to like an online post or not.

Group activities

Working in small groups, pupils can think about what the term 'honesty' means. Write down pupils' ideas to be shared with the rest of the class. Use the outcome of the activity to steer the questions in the follow-up activity. Ask pupils to hold up their whiteboards to show 'yes' or 'no' responses to a range of questions, such as:

• Have you ever lied about where you have been? For example, have you said that you have been to a place in the world that you haven't? Why were you not truthful?

Depending on the age and sensitivity of the class, these questions could be asked at the teacher's discretion and followed up with questions to prompt further discussion, such as:

• Have you ever lied about your age to gain access to an app?
• Has anyone ever been nasty to you online? If so, how did it make you feel? How did you respond?
• Are you aware of friends/family editing pictures before posting them on social media? If so, why do you think they edited their pictures? What impact can this have on self-esteem and self-worth?

Teacher notes

It is important that, before these activities commence, pupils are reminded of classroom rules such as confidentiality. The questions asked and the follow-up discussions should be steered by teachers' own professional judgement.

Each question could be further explored to elicit feelings, emotions and reasoning from pupils, with the teacher acting as the role model with model answers. At the end of the activity, the teacher may ask pupils to rate how honest they think they are and to consider how they could improve their honesty. The teacher may ask questions such as:

• Did you look at other people's answers before you showed yours?

- If you did the activity again and closed your eyes, would you answer differently?
- How does honesty affect how we feel?
- When we are honest, it gives us an internal sense of pride. When we are dishonest, how does that make you feel? When someone is dishonest to you, how does that make you feel?

Challenge

The teacher may ask questions such as:

- Is being honest always the right thing to do?
- Can honesty be both positive and negative?
- Are there any circumstances where dishonesty online may be acceptable?

These questions can provide an opportunity to discuss social etiquette: when you tell a 'good' lie because you do not like what somebody is wearing or because you are helping to plan a surprise. To encourage discussion, the teacher may share a scenario with pupils, such as:

Your friend is wearing their favourite outfit that they have been saving up for a long time to buy. They send you a photo wearing it and ask for your opinion. You really don't like it, but how should you respond?

Reflection

To be completed independently as a final activity.

- What does honesty mean to me?
- Rate your level of honesty in real life from 0-10 (0 = least honest, 10 = most honest).
- Rate your level of honesty online from 0-10 (0 = least honest, 10 = most honest).
- How do the two scores compare? If one score is higher, why? What could you do to improve how truthful you are?
- How does it make you feel when you are honest? How does it make you feel when you are dishonest?

PUTTING THE THEORY INTO PRACTICE: 'WALK THE LINE' ASSEMBLY IDEA FOR KS2

This idea has been adapted from the Jubilee Centre for Character and Virtues' character curriculum.[61] The aim is to encourage pupils to think about taking responsibility for who they are online.

Entry music: *Walk the Line*, Johnny Cash.

- The internet is an amazing tool and we can use it to do lots of fun things. The teacher may ask pupils to share some of the things they enjoy doing on the internet.

- Most of us are not just passive users of the internet (watching videos, looking at information, etc.) but also active users. We might post comments, share content or talk to people online.

- This is why we are responsible for the ways in which we interact online. People online can be kind (e.g. sending supportive messages and comments to people they might not be able to see in person), generous (e.g. donating to charity or fundraising for charity) and courageous (e.g. standing up to or reporting inappropriate content). However, just like offline, people online can also be unkind (e.g. posting mean comments), dishonest (e.g. creating fake profiles) and cowardly (e.g. not reporting or calling out inappropriate behaviour).

- The teacher may show this video, which won Trend Micro's 2011 'What's Your Story?' internet safety video competition, as a springboard to discuss online behaviour: youtu.be/SdC7iBpD8Sk.

- The teacher might want to mark a line on the floor with masking tape and have a positive side and a negative side, like in the video. The teacher may then ask pupils to think about what behaviours or actions should be on the right side of the line, and what behaviours or actions should be on the wrong side. Relatedly, the teacher may want to ask pupils: how do we ensure that we, and our friends, are on the right side of the line? What virtues will we need to show?

- We are responsible for the type of people we are online. We need to make sure our words and actions online reflect the type of people we want to be.

> **Reflection**: Can you think about a time when you have been on the wrong side of the line? What can you do to make it right?

OBJECTIVE 6: NURTURE DIGITAL WISDOM

Pupils need to possess wisdom that enables them to act with deliberation and discernment, and to do the right thing at the right time, when using digital technologies.

Cultivating digital wisdom in pupils is the ultimate goal of our digital citizenship education framework. If pupils develop digital wisdom, they are somewhat futureproofed for their digital lives after they leave school. They know how to make the right decisions at the right time in the digital world, especially when no one is watching. This goal is unlikely to ever be fully realised because we are all constantly refining our digital wisdom, as and when we face new ethical dilemmas and other challenging situations.

Showing digital wisdom involves making decisions and judgements about how to apply our character in specific situations and contexts mediated by digital technologies – what might be called digital good sense. As such, digital wisdom is the expression of autonomous decision-making and virtuous action. It is also the moderator of the other virtues, which is why it might be best considered a meta virtue. It helps users of digital technologies to decide, for example, when to be honest to a teacher or when to be loyal to a friend.

Digital wisdom cannot be taught in a traditional sense and is often not developed through direct instruction. Schools can encourage their pupils to be digitally wise but cannot *make* them, nor should they seek to do so. Teachers can show pupils exemplars of digital wisdom but they cannot force pupils to possess this quality, nor can they assess whether, or how, pupils will show digital wisdom in practice when using digital technologies. This quality is developed primarily through experience. No one can ever be fully digitally wise: we are all learning how to use digital technologies with critical discernment and in a way that contributes to our own and others' flourishing. Likewise, no one is born digitally wise: it is a quality that is honed over time and with conscious and continuous hard work.

Although teachers cannot 'teach' pupils to be digitally wise, they can introduce educational activities aimed at cultivating the components of this quality. The more learning that is directed at these components, the more likely that pupils will know what digital wisdom is, why it matters in their lives and the lives of others, and how to spot situations that need a wise decision. The following components of digital wisdom, taken from the work of the Jubilee Centre for Character and Virtues,[62] can be targeted through deliberate educational activities and approaches.

- **Digital wisdom literacy**: an understanding of the nature of different virtues, and of the contexts and ways in which they can be deployed when using digital technologies.

- **Digital wisdom reasoning**: evaluation of and ability to prioritise different virtues when using digital technologies, particularly when experiencing moral dilemmas dependent on context.

- **Digital wisdom self-reflection**: reflection on and ability to navigate one's own biases, perspectives and emotions, and those of others, when using digital technologies.

- **Digital wisdom motivation**: the desire to act online with different virtues, in line with a vision of the digital world underpinned by principles of the common good.

Teachers can draw on the work of the Jubilee Centre and other organisations to target each of these components. For example, narratives could be used to enhance digital wisdom literacy, or exemplars used to show how others have demonstrated digital wisdom motivation. Another example, outlined below, is using moral dilemmas to introduce pupils to the idea that they must employ reason when faced with situations that may be hard to navigate from an ethical perspective.

PUTTING THE THEORY INTO PRACTICE: AN EXPLORATION OF MORAL DILEMMAS WITH SECONDARY PUPILS

It is clear that digitally mediated interactions and activities have become an integral part of children's daily lives. We cannot simply assume that because today's children were born in the digital age, they will automatically know how to navigate the digital landscape, and how to act and behave virtuously in a respectful and appropriate manner online.

It is a false proxy to assume that because pupils use digital technologies a lot, they possess the skills, knowledge and values necessary to use these technologies correctly and sensibly. Relatedly, we cannot assume that they will acquire these skills, knowledge and values by osmosis.

There is a real disconnect between how some pupils act in person and how they present themselves and act online. Teachers need to address this issue, educating pupils about how their behaviour and actions online have equal status and consequences to their behaviour and actions in person. Teachers also need to explain to pupils how their online activities leave a traceable legacy that can impact on their future lives.

In the UK, schools are now required to teach pupils about online behaviour through the new statutory module of PSHE called 'relationships and sex education' (RSE). This is in line with the DfE's guidance on 'keeping children safe in education',[63] which places emphasis on contextual safeguarding (that is, anything that is extra-familial and that a child is exposed to outside the family unit).

If we want pupils to demonstrate good character and make virtuous decisions online, educators should expect them to act like this in the offline world first. Making virtuous choices must be habitual, automatic, programmed and ingrained. Only then is there a real chance of encouraging pupils to act in this way online when no one else is looking.

One way to help pupils act more virtuously, supporting them to make the right decisions at the right time and for the right reasons (in person and online), is by using moral dilemmas. Moral dilemmas allow pupils to develop their moral compasses by exploring a real-life scenario that they may one day face.

Moral dilemma 1

This dilemma is to be explored in a personal development lesson, PSHE lesson or tutor time. The aim is for pupils to understand that expressing hate, racism, sexism or violence is not acceptable and can harm others. We all have a responsibility to stand up and speak out against bad behaviour online.

Here is the dilemma:

You have witnessed people making negative and hurtful comments about someone in your class online. You know that a lot of people have seen these comments and have heard people talking about the victim and laughing about the comments that have been made. You realise that the victim is not in school that day and have heard someone saying that this is probably because of the direct messages that were sent to them. You have not sent any of the messages or commented, so you do not want to get involved.

Class discussion points

The teacher may ask pupils to discuss with the person next to them the following questions. The teacher can then ask pupils to share their responses.

- What do you do next?
- How can we take action here?
- How might the victim feel? What impact may their feelings have on them?
- What advice would you give to the victim?
- What advice would you give to the perpetrator?

The teacher could then share the following video for the #TogetherAgainstHate campaign and facilitate class discussion to focus on the key messages: youtu.be/vP-CCBKCRwk. The teacher could use the structured talk prompts below when asking pupils to give their different viewpoints or responses.

Moral dilemma 2

Much of what we see posted on social media platforms such as Instagram, TikTok and Facebook is edited to present a false image of perfection. Social media profiles now act as a 'highlight reel' and very rarely share the challenges or low points that we all face in life. This is problematic in many ways and can make people feel their life is not good enough, when what they are comparing themselves to is not entirely real.

Here is the second dilemma:

You post an edited picture of yourself on social media where you have whitened your teeth, made yourself look slimmer, removed any spots and posed next to an expensive car. Lots of your followers comment about how great you look and how happy you seem. You receive a message from an old school friend telling you how happy they are for you that your life has turned out this way. Meanwhile, they go on to tell you that things are not great for them and that they have been feeling depressed. In truth, your life is not as exciting as the one you present on social media. In reality, you actually feel insecure and down.

Class discussion points

The teacher may ask pupils to discuss with the person next to them the following questions. The teacher can then ask pupils to share their responses.

- Do you respond to your old school friend by telling them the truth?
- Why do people present themselves in this way on social media?
- Is this a positive or negative aspect of social media?
- How do you feel about edited or photoshopped pictures on social media?
- What impact can these types of pictures have on people?

The teacher could then share the following video, titled 'This is how social media is destroying your life', and facilitate class discussion to focus on the key messages: youtu.be/e2Tq2gvGt80. The teacher could use the structured talk prompts below when asking pupils to give their different viewpoints or responses.

PUTTING THE THEORY INTO PRACTICE: AN ASSEMBLY FOR KS4 ON USING TECHNOLOGY WISELY

This idea has been adapted from the Jubilee Centre for Character and Virtues' character curriculum.[64] The aim is to explore how to use technology wisely and how to develop digital virtues that enhance effective integration of digital technologies into daily life.

Preparation and materials: The 'How technology tries to hack your brain' video from BBC Newsnight – youtu.be/WoIufBVLDvM.

- The teacher may introduce the topic and underline what technological change means in the digital age where we are more connected than ever.

- The teacher may pose the following questions to pupils for discussion:

  – How might the use of digital technologies harm or be detrimental to us?

  – What concerns do adults have about young people's use of digital technologies?

  – Are their concerns valid or out of proportion?

- The teacher may share some statistics about how many young people use social media and other online platforms. In addition, the teacher may pose the following questions:

  – What are the different ways that digital technologies might 'hook' people in?

– Why is this potentially harmful?

- The teacher may show the video above and pose the following questions for discussion:

  – What concerns does this video raise over the use of digital technologies by teenagers?

  – What concerns you the most?

  – Which of the issues discussed most impinge on your life?

- A lot of discussion around digital technologies relates to evaluating the negative effects of their use on our lives. However, these technologies do present many opportunities to develop virtues, both through the cultivation of character and in resisting the control and impact that technology has on us. To explore this issue, the teacher may pose the following questions for discussion:

  – Does the use of digital technologies like smartphones and the internet give you a net gain or a net loss in your life?

  – Which virtues do these technologies allow you to develop and how might you go about identifying and developing virtues?

Reflection

Use of digital technologies is growing and statistics show that we spend a lot of time online. The teacher may ask pupils to reflect on the question: how do you feel about the amount of time you spend online?

PUTTING THE THEORY INTO PRACTICE: LINKING DIGITAL WISDOM TO SELF-REWARD AND SELF-SANCTIONING

Nurturing digital wisdom could be an extension of teaching younger pupils to self-reward and self-sanction. Games can support the development of this from a very young age, by encouraging pupils not to rely on an adult or someone else to tell them 'well done', but rather to feel satisfied for making the right choice themselves. This can be developed over time, first by being modelled by adults and then by pupils praising one another.

The suggested learning intentions of this activity are:

- To take control of our own choices and how this makes us feel.
- To take pride in our actions and show respect for ourselves and others through self-control.

Classroom activity

Working in groups or independently, pupils think about what wisdom means and what 'being wise' may look like in a range of offline scenarios. The teacher may ask pupils to share examples to facilitate further discussion, highlighting why the example shows wisdom.

Examples of scenarios include:

- I am going to go to bed early tonight as I have school tomorrow.
- I want to eat healthily and so I am not going to have chocolate.
- I do not know how to do this piece of work and so I am going to ask my teacher.

The teacher may then ask the following questions for discussion:

- How does it make you feel when you make the right judgement call?
- Do you think about the repercussions of making a wrong choice? Does this steer your decision?

The teacher may then present an online scenario to pupils – for example, sharing a screenshot of unkind online comments from social media platforms such as Twitter, Instagram or Facebook. These could be fictional or taken from examples that are relevant at the time.

Ask pupils how they would respond if they received comments like these. Pupils may be asked to discuss first in groups and then as a class in order to elicit different responses. The teacher may record good choices on the board for all to see (e.g. ignoring the comments, reporting them, etc.).

Next, the teacher may provide groups of pupils with a card that presents multiple online scenarios (including scenarios that may be pertinent to the school/class at the time) and ask pupils what they would do in those scenarios. For example:

- You receive an email to click on a link to receive money.
- You receive a Facebook request from a friend's duplicate account.
- You see some mean comments online about a celebrity.
- You receive an email to say that someone has hacked into your account and you need to share your password in order to reset the account.
- Someone sends you a threatening email/text/message.

The teacher can repeatedly ask pupils how they can show wisdom and how it feels to make a right choice. Each group may be asked to present their response to the rest of the class. The teacher can praise the groups when they make the right choices and pupils may be encouraged to praise one another.

PUTTING THE THEORY INTO PRACTICE: THE RECIPE FOR DIGITAL WISDOM

Digital wisdom requires certain character traits to be shown. In this activity, the teacher may ask pupils – individually, in groups or as a class – to write a recipe identifying the key ingredients of being 'digitally wise'.

The suggested learning intentions are:

- To explore the virtues required to act wisely online.
- To explore what being digitally wise means and how it looks to act virtuously online (giving younger children examples as a scaffold, while encouraging older children to think hard).

It is important to differentiate here according to age. Younger children could be given virtues on cards and physically choose different virtues to add to their recipe. The teacher could talk about the virtues and ask pupils to give examples of what they mean, referring back to how these virtues are used online. The key is to encourage pupils to develop the language associated with virtues and to overcome the disconnect between behaviour in the offline world and behaviour online.

What will the ingredients be? The teacher may ask pupils to think in groups about which virtues are important online – perhaps empathy and compassion are deemed as valuable ingredients in being digitally wise. For example:

- One cup of empathy.
- Two cups of compassion.
- Served on a thick base of honesty.
- Finished with good judgement.

Once the ingredients have been decided upon, the teacher may talk to pupils about how these ingredients could be adapted according to the context, just as ingredients for a cake can be altered. In some situations, people may need more empathy; in others, more self-control. To make this activity more challenging, the teacher may give pupils scenarios and ask them to decide the amount of each ingredient required.

For older children, the teacher could ask them what virtues they would rely upon to steer them through the following scenarios and why.

- You are online and see that someone is receiving nasty comments. What do you do?
- You have received an unpleasant comment. How do you react?
- You have been asked to share inappropriate material. What do you do?

Asking pupils why they have chosen specific virtues and tipped the balance in certain ways will allow the teacher to discuss further scenarios. For example, 'If you responded like that and then X happened, what would you do?'

PART 3
DIGITAL RISKS AND OPPORTUNITIES

INTRODUCTION

In the third part of this book, we begin by providing a deeper overview of the digital risks and opportunities that schools should address through their formal and informal curricula. First we cover five risks relating to abuse, crime, privacy, mistrust and wellbeing. Then we cover five opportunities relating to learning, connection, leisure, employment and citizenship. Although digital technologies are constantly evolving and this can bring new risks and opportunities, we believe these 10 broad categories will endure into the foreseeable future. As such, they should be seen as pillars around which the content of a whole-school approach to digital citizenship education may be built. Such an approach is discussed at the end of part 3. This is when we provide a table for teaching digital citizenship education, both in line with the components of this form of education, as established earlier in the book, and in ways that relate to specific digital risks and opportunities.

The risks and opportunities that will be discussed echo previous typologies developed for mapping the positive and negative impact of digital technologies on younger users and society at large. These include, for example, Sonia Livingstone et al's classification of online risks and opportunities,[65] as well as a recently updated classification of online risks developed by the pan-European project Children Online: Research and Evidence (CORE).[66] However, although providing a typology of digital risks and opportunities is a useful exercise, what is trickier to predict is the exact nature of the different issues that relate to each of the risks we present, and how prevalent these issues may be year on year. Some issues – like cyberbullying, a form of online abuse – have been around since the invention of the internet. Others, such as image-based sexual abuse, are more recent and have arisen since the invention of the smartphone. The opportunities that digital technologies present can also be hard to predict, as pupils are required to develop knowledge and an understanding of these technologies in ways that respond to how they learn, work and live.

IMPORTANT RELATED PUBLICATIONS

The table in part 1 of this book (see page 21) lists a number of important publications that relate to the theme of digital citizenship education. The following publications, drawn from this list, particularly focus on digital risks and opportunities.

- *Education for a Connected World* (2020), published by the UK Council for Internet Safety, provides a framework to equip children and young people for their digital lives. This comprehensive publication offers lots of advice and resources for schools linked primarily to risks, including self-image and identity, online relationships, online reputation and cyberbullying. It also contains very helpful tables that show what pupils should know at different ages. It can be accessed here: bit.ly/3KcKmvK

- *Teaching Online Safety in School* (2019) is published by the Department for Education and consists of non-statutory guidance that supports schools to teach pupils how to stay safe online in the context of studying new and existing subjects. It can be accessed here: bit.ly/3hDdcZX

- *Relationships Education, Relationships and Sex Education (RSE) and Health Education* (2019) was published by the DfE and consists of statutory guidance for primary and secondary schools on relationships education, RSE and health education. Many of the issues addressed in the guidance relate to pupils' lives online. It can be accessed here: bit.ly/3MprDz2

In the following pages, we use case studies to discuss each of the risks and opportunities that are central to our approach to digital citizenship education. The case studies are designed to bring the reader closer to the real-life (and in some cases everyday) risks and opportunities experienced by children and young people in the digital age. After each case study, we provide a short general description of the related risk or opportunity. In the risks section, we focus on some of the issues associated with each risk. We give just a short overview of each of these issues; all the risks (and associated issues) and opportunities are large topics in themselves, which is why whole books have been devoted to exploring them.

Although we discuss each risk and opportunity separately, it should be clarified that the risks presented by digital technologies, as well as their opportunities, often overlap in practice. Think, for example, of the negative impact the internet can have on mental health because of different forms of online abuse, or because of criminal behaviour such as online grooming. Or think of the extent to which online abuse such as cyberstalking, or criminal behaviour such as identity theft and fraud, are exacerbated online by the implications of the internet in terms of privacy. Finally, although all the following risks and opportunities were pertinent as we wrote the book, they will likely manifest themselves in various ways over time. This is why it is important that teachers are aware of the changing nature of digital technologies. Undoubtedly, the technology or app of the day will impact on how we teach about being a citizen in the digital age.

DIGITAL RISKS

In this section, we detail each of the five overarching digital risks, along with various issues related to them. The table below provides an overview of the five risks, including definitions and the associated issues.

Risk	Definition	Issues
Abuse	The use of digital technologies to abuse others.	Cyberbullying, image-based sexual abuse, trolling.
Crime	The use of digital technologies to commit crime.	Online grooming, extremism, theft/fraud/scams/phishing.
Privacy	The use of digital technologies to invade and exploit others' privacy.	Data-tracking, digital footprint.
Mistrust	The use of digital technologies to increase mistrust in society.	Misinformation, distorted identities, plagiarism.
Wellbeing	The use of digital technologies in a way that reduces the mental and/or physical wellbeing of users.	Screen time, inappropriate content, depression and self-harm.

ABUSE
The use of digital technologies to abuse others.

CASE STUDY

'Like' culture now holds sway over many children and young people, especially as trends show they are accessing social media from an increasingly young age. Some children aged as young as seven have become accustomed to not only receiving but also chasing likes for things they say or post online. This does not stop when the screen shuts down, as it is becoming increasingly evident to teachers that many are starting to need this affirmation in the offline world, mirroring their online behaviour in the classroom as well as in the playground.

Children and young people verbalise the increasing pressures on them to fit in with their peers, replicating the 'want' and sometimes 'need' to be liked both online and offline. Indeed, school staff often report a gradual shift in the views of pupils, commenting that they can almost see invisible likes hanging over pupils' heads as their online accounts seem to morph into how they, and others, see themselves in and around school.

This, in turn, is encouraging popularity contests within the playground, replicating the online culture of influencers, as the most 'liked' pupils determine what is popular and what is not. The need to receive approval on social media platforms has exacerbated the impact on those who do not receive online or in-playground likes, thus affecting their self-esteem. While some pupils rise in popularity, others plummet and receive unkind comments. At times, it feels like forms of online abuse such as trolling have broken through the screen and the impact is being felt in the classroom.

Constant negative comments online can easily become bullying, which can spill into the classroom and on to the playground. This can manifest itself in a range of ways and feelings, from depression to anger. Some children have to undergo counselling from trained practitioners to support them with their anxiety and depleting feeling of self-worth. This is why it is important that pupils understand it is so much easier and quicker to damage one's own self-esteem online, and much harder to build this back up.

At the root of this growing problem is the simple fact that children are finding it increasingly hard to differentiate between the online world and the offline world around them. Teachers often describe how the seemingly sanction-free world of the internet fuels pupils' perception that online behaviours can be mirrored in the offline world. Children are struggling with this confusion between online and offline behaviour, as their online behaviour often goes unchallenged. Online profiles and actions can become more and more extreme as children delve into grown-up virtual worlds. As a result, incidents reported in schools around online activity sometimes uncover personae that are unrecognisable from the children known to schools.

Post-lockdown, in an inner-city primary school, a Year 6 boy brought an online disagreement into the classroom the following day. The child was so caught up in what was happening on the screen that it extended into the offline world and led to real feelings of anger and physical threats. Anger and other negative emotions are such a driving force for online incidents spilling into schools; addressing this problem requires work aimed at developing pupils' ability to regulate and reflect on their own emotions.

Of course, not all incidents are quite as dramatic. However, primary school playgrounds nowadays can, at times, be mistaken for social media communities coming to life as interactions that happen online in pupils' bedrooms continue the next day in school. And, just like the online forums they are growing to imitate, so schoolyards now have their fair share of likes, influencers and, sadly, trolls and bullies crawling out of the internet's shadows.

Many children, by the time they reach the age of 13, will have witnessed some form of online abuse. They may not be the victims of the abuse, but they will have likely observed unkind comments being posted on apps and/or social media platforms. Given the prevalence and severity of online abuse, it is not surprising that it is one of the greatest concerns of parents, teachers and pupils.

We adopt a maximal definition of abuse in this book, encompassing:

- **Frequency**: the abuse might be a one-off or happen repeatedly over a long period of time. One-off abuse can have dramatic but shorter-term negative effects on victims, whereas longer-term sustained attacks are likely to have a more significant impact on victims' health and wellbeing. Abuse attacks online might occur sporadically or at more regular intervals.

- **Severity**: abuse attacks might be viewed on a scale from lower-level teasing to deliberately hurtful and targeted cruelty. Attacks are likely to be seen as more abusive if they are intentional, repeated, undertaken anonymously, involve an imbalance of power and/or more than one abuser, and if the abuse takes place on and offline.[67] The severity of the abuse also depends partly on how the victim responds to the attacks, on their own personality and on the support network they have around them.

- **Deliberate**: actions and communications can be misinterpreted. This is especially the case with digitally mediated (particularly text-based) communication. More specifically, the absence of visual cues (such as body language) and audible cues (such as tone) mean it is sometimes hard to determine the intention or meaning behind an online post or form of communication. Research shows content that is not meant to be abusive may be interpreted as hurtful.[68] For digitally mediated activities/communications to be considered abusive, there should be a deliberate intention to hurt or harm someone.

- **Using digital technologies**: the abuse is carried out through digital technologies, at least partially. This might involve using a single platform such as Snapchat, Instagram or WhatsApp, or multiple platforms. Digitally mediated abuse might also be undertaken alongside more traditional face-to-face forms of abuse.

In short, in this book we use 'abuse' as a catch-all term to describe any use of digital technologies with the intention of being deliberately cruel, unkind and uncaring to someone else. This includes, most prominently, cyberbullying, image-based sexual abuse and trolling, which are described later in this section. The following list details other forms of online abuse that are not discussed further in this book, but may be connected to cyberbullying, image-based sexual abuse and trolling.

- **Doxing**: sharing someone's personal information with the intention of getting them harassed.

- **Astroturfing**: making coordinated efforts to amplify abuse so it appears as though it originates from a grassroots source.

- **Dog-piling**: a collective group undertaking an abusive attack on a target or targets.

- **Cyberstalking**: the sustained and repeated use of abusive or harassing behaviour online.
- **Deepfake**: manipulation of images/content to make it appear as though someone has said or done something abusive.
- **Dog-whistling**: using coded messages or language with a double meaning to abuse someone or an organisation.
- **Exclusion**: deliberately leaving someone out of a group.
- **Flaming**: similar to trolling, a direct attack on a victim in order to incite them into online fights.
- **Fraping**: stealing someone else's account/profile to post abusive comments.

According to cross-comparative research conducted in Europe and published in 2018,[69] teenagers who experience cyberbullying are 2.3 times more likely to self-harm, 2.1 times more likely to exhibit suicidal behaviour and 2.5 times more likely to attempt suicide.

Issue 1: Cyberbullying
The use of digital technologies to support deliberate abusive behaviour, by an individual or group, with the intention of hurting others.

Several studies show that 10-40% of children and young people report being victims of cyberbullying, in the UK and elsewhere.

Cyberbullying can be a blight on many children's and young people's lives, causing long-lasting mental distress and detrimental effects to their wellbeing.[70] Since the 1990s, commentators have consistently considered the topic in books, articles and news features. These publications have responded to many tragic cases of teenage suicide linked to online harassment. Debates range in the literature about how cyberbullying should be defined and conceptualised, and about its prevalence.[71] The reported rates of cyberbullying vary across studies depending on how it is defined,[72] the age of respondents and the timeframe over which they were asked.[73] Academic interest in cyberbullying is on the increase. In 2015, for example, there were 3.5 new academic articles a week on cyberbullying, of which 9% had a focus on interventions to reduce or prevent it.[74]

Cyberbullying is a perennial concern for schools and one that many teachers believe has most affected their role in recent years. Teachers are now expected to manage bullying that has taken place online and out of school, as well as face-to-face bullying occurring on school grounds. Individual instances of bullying can quickly become significant as messages are shared around school, causing maximum upset or harm to the victims. As a result, teachers, who are unable to impose rules on their pupils' internet use overnight and in the home, are required to focus primarily on character-based strategies to counter the issue.

Issue 2: Image-based sexual abuse
Sharing of private sexual materials without consent and for the purposes of abuse or blackmail.

> According to a 2018 meta-analysis of studies conducted with 110,000 teenagers worldwide,[75] one in seven teens had reported sending 'sexts' and one in four had reported receiving 'sexts'.

Although image-based sexual abuse is more commonly known as revenge porn and sexting, the term 'image-based sexual abuse' better captures the nature and harms of non-consensual creation and distribution of private sexual images. More precisely, the term captures the broad range of different practices perpetrated by abusers and conveys the nature and extent of the abuse, as well as the possible harms suffered by victims.[76] Although an exact description of what constitutes private sexual images is hard to pin down, the following definition adapted from the 2015 UK government guidance is useful.

> *... private materials are those showing anything not usually seen in public. Sexual material not only covers images that show the pubic region, but anything that a reasonable person would consider to be sexual, so this could be a picture of someone who is engaged in sexual behaviour or posing in a sexually provocative way.*[77]

Image-based sexual abuse is defined in this book as the sharing of private sexual materials without consent and for the specific purpose of causing distress or embarrassment. As such, it has also been linked to blackmail.

For some children and young people, sexting has become normalised. More precisely, the reasons they might give for sharing sexual images with others include wanting to start a new relationship, wanting to please their boyfriend or girlfriend, hoping to elicit positive comments about their body, or being pressurised into it.

> The charity Refuge found in 2020 that around one in seven young women had received threats to share intimate pictures or videos.[78]

The UK government has been developing new legislation to make it easier to prosecute instances of revenge porn and sexting.[79] Since 2015, those found guilty may be fined and sentenced to up to two years in prison.

Image-based sexual abuse is a common problem in many schools, particularly when pupils do not understand the need to protect their online identity or the consequences of private pictures being shared. Sexting is a bigger problem than revenge porn and involves pupils who often become victims, because they share sexual images privately with ex-boyfriends/girlfriends that are later shared via social media platforms or messaging services. Teachers, who are called on to support the victims of sexting, are expected to reprimand culprits and teach students about the possible consequences of sharing sexual images.

> The Centre for Strategy & Evaluation Services in the UK found in 2019 that online trolls present the following indicative psychological traits: narcissism, psychopathy, Machiavellianism and everyday sadism.[80]

Issue 3: Trolling
Posting an insulting or abusive message on a public forum or social media platform with the main aim of annoying someone and/or gaining attention.

> According to the Centre for Strategy & Evaluation Services,[81] 1% of internet users in the UK had been trolled online at least once over the past 12 months in 2019. This went up to 5% for respondents aged 16-24.

Trolling differs from cyberbullying in one important aspect. Cyberbullying is generally directed at individuals. Trolling, by contrast, is generally directed at online communities and carried out within open online settings (where interaction, discussion and debate are encouraged), including social media platforms and online forums, discussion and comment threads, and online gaming chat forums. Often, trolling is undertaken by users who are anonymous. Trolls seek to garner attention from users – they might be racist, sexist, hurtful or use profanity to do so. Relatedly, trolls aim to maximise upset and hurt online by starting arguments and posting controversial comments, deliberately seeking to promote hatred.

Trolls may have one or more of the following motivations:

- To bring attention to themselves.
- To deliberately hurt other people.
- To cause destruction and upset.
- To put people off participating/interacting online.
- To amuse themselves.
- To target a particular audience.

Trolling tends to be less of an immediate issue for schools and teachers, as the abuse is not generally aimed at specific individuals known to the troll, but at unknown individuals or groups. Teachers should still seek to detect pupils who are engaging in trolling and find out their motivations. They should also teach about trolling in the digital citizenship curriculum and as part of a general effort to reduce trolling online.

CRIME
The use of digital technologies to commit crime.

CASE STUDY

During lockdown in 2020, online apps became a form of entertainment for many children within the home. One app that saw a rise in usage, especially among younger pupils, was TikTok. Hours upon hours were spent making up and recreating dances and other creative montages. In fact, TikTok became so popular that some schools even broadcast messages through the platform. However, with this popularity came the potential for crime such as online grooming, especially with the rise in children accessing apps in ways that were largely unmonitored.

This was the case when a seven-year-old pupil in the North of England innocently posted photographs and dance routines to share with her friends on TikTok. Unbeknown to her parents, she had lied about her age when setting up her profile and enabled the chat function within the app, while keeping her profile open to the public. A young male befriended her and over time started to send her naked photographs through the chat facility, requesting naked photos in return and lying about his age and motives for following her.

As the pupil's primary school had taught her about internet safety, she knew how to report the person through the function within the app. However, the perpetrator set up other fake accounts and continued to pursue the child, who had unwittingly given out her mobile phone number. Incessant overnight phone calls, texts and photos followed, leaving the child scared to report anything in case the offender knew where she lived or went to school.

'Post-lockdown, we saw a real surge in the numbers of children accessing apps such as TikTok and YouTube,' said the headteacher who dealt with the incident. 'Children, from a far younger age, were posting videos and pictures, unaware of the potential dangers … It is only too easy for children to become embroiled in dangerous and even criminal activity online without any warning signs to parents or teachers. Only through highly skilled school staff picking up on the fact that the child seemed extremely tired and withdrawn was this incident reported and thankfully resolved.'

With the continuous evolution of technology comes the continuous release of new apps. And, although many are aimed at the adult market, with recommended age limits, children are increasingly downloading and using them. On the face of it, many apps seem 'harmless', designed for innocuous games or videos. However, they may have additional features that allow users to chat and interact, and these features can create the greatest risks since they are often unknown or misunderstood by adults, who may be unable to monitor the activity of their children or support them when needed.

So, how to protect our children against the ever-evolving dangers amplified by digital technologies? As the case of the seven-year-old pupil demonstrates, it is not enough to rely on safeguards within apps and computer programs, nor to think that we can truly monitor everything children are accessing on their devices at all times. Instead, we need to build an on-board safeguarding mechanism within children themselves. We need to encourage them to question who they are speaking to and have the confidence to ask for help.

As the headteacher from the primary school explains, 'Within school we had previously taught a wide range of internet safety awareness and had worked with the full range of stakeholders to develop a vision for digital wisdom. It is the framework that was developed with the children that the child remembered and put to good use, in order to avoid a potentially disastrous situation.'

Instead of trying to tackle individual issues, a switch to proactively teaching key character qualities such as wisdom, courage, self-esteem and confidence could equip pupils with the tools required to navigate most dangers by themselves before these dangers become a problem. At the same time, teaching pupils how to regulate their own emotions and not panic when under pressure can set them up for a lifetime of using the internet more confidently.

Crime is a broad term that in this book covers any online activities that threaten children's and young people's safety and security in the short and longer term. Some online crimes, such as grooming and extremism, could put children and young people in immediate danger. Others, such as fraud and scams, could have longer-term effects on their mental health and sense of security.

Digital technologies have made it easier for crimes such as grooming, extremism and fraud to take place. This is because of the affordances of the internet, such as the ability to communicate anonymously, to connect with people all over the world instantly and to interact with others easily on a mass scale.

To help protect pupils from crime, schools should ensure that they realise the internet is largely unregulated and some of its technical features make it easier for criminals to commit crimes. Consequently, pupils need to be watchful, alert and to self-regulate their actions. Schools should also teach pupils about the most common online crimes and how these may put them in danger. They should be helped to spot the signs of online crime that might put them at risk, and taught about the negative and sometimes serious consequences of different forms of digital crime on individuals and society more broadly. In short, it is important that schools support pupils to become wise users of digital technologies. This means helping them to become more critically aware and to autonomously question the motivations of those with whom they interact online.

Issue 4: Online grooming
A deliberate attempt to build a relationship and emotional connection with a child or young person so that they can be manipulated, exploited and/or abused.

> The NSPCC found in 2020 that 4% of 11- to 17-year-olds in the UK had sent, received or been asked to send sexual messages to an adult. This figure more than doubled to 9% among children who feel lonely, unhappy, are introvert and rely on social media.

Since verbal and written communications through digital technologies became the norm, there has been an increased risk of children and young people being befriended online by strangers in order to be taken advantage of for sexual purposes. This is commonly known as online grooming. Within online settings, it is possible for groomers to act anonymously, hide behind their screens and use different techniques to entice children into communicating with them. Groomers often set up fake profiles and pretend to be someone they are not, in order to build up trust with potential victims and avoid detection by the police. Common methods of building trust with children and young people include complimenting them, offering gifts and pretending to share common interests. Another tactic pursued by groomers is to try to isolate their victims from their friends and families and to make them feel dependent; this gives the groomer power and control over their victims. Once trust has been established, the groomer may try to get the child or young person to talk about their sexual experiences, send sexual videos or pictures of themselves and possibly even meet up.

Online groomers will operate on sites that are popular with children and young people, including gaming sites, social media platforms and specialist forums. The NSPCC suggests that children and young people might display the following signs if they are being groomed.[82]

- Being very secretive about how they are spending their time, including when online.
- Having an older boyfriend or girlfriend.
- Having money or new things like clothes and mobile phones that they cannot or will not explain.
- Underage drinking or drug-taking.
- Spending more or less time online or on their devices.
- Being upset, withdrawn or distressed.
- Sexualised behaviour, language or an understanding of sex that is not appropriate for their age.
- Spending more time away from home or going missing for periods of time.

A new law was introduced in 2017 by the UK government, giving the police the power to charge adults who send a sexual message to a child in England and Wales.

In a 2018 survey of 40,000 pupils in the UK, the London Grid for Learning found that two in five young people had never told anyone about the worst thing that had happened to them online, meaning that many instances of online grooming will not be reported.

Schools need to make all pupils aware of the dangers of online grooming. They should look out for signs that children are being groomed, especially when it comes to children who spend a lot of time alone or on their smartphone. Finally, they should teach children not to trust everyone they meet online and to have the courage to report communication that concerns them.

Issue 5: Extremism

The use of digital technologies to recruit, communicate with and mobilise children and young people to oppose fundamental values, including democracy, the rule of law, individual liberty, and respect and tolerance for different faiths and beliefs.

> In 2019, the UK Commission for Countering Extremism found that just under half (45%) of those who had witnessed extremism had seen it online.

> As reported by Twitter, during the first half of 2019 the social media company removed more than 100,000 accounts promoting terrorism, and locked or suspended more than 50,000 accounts for breaching policy guidelines on violent extremism.

Online extremism has been poorly defined, making it hard for researchers to identify the risk to children and young people and assess its prevalence. The UK government defines extremism as 'opposition to our fundamental values, including democracy, the rule of law, individual liberty and the mutual respect and tolerance of different faiths and beliefs'.[83] Extremism differs from terrorism – it refers to a belief system rather than the use or threat of violence to advance a particular cause. However, the two are linked, as extremism can lead to radicalisation and terrorist activities, although this link is not well understood. While extremism occurs online and offline, the internet has enabled the spread of extremism, making it easier to attract younger people to specific belief systems. Extremists exploit digital technologies to set up groups that can be hard to detect. They also use mainstream platforms like Facebook and YouTube to post videos and comments, as these can attract a larger audience.

The use of digital technologies can contribute to extremism in the following ways.

- **Recruitment**: reaching children and young people and attracting them to extremist viewpoints.
- **Socialisation**: socialising children and young people to think certain extremist viewpoints are normal and acceptable.

- **Networking**: drawing children and young people into groups of extremists across the world.
- **Mobilisation**: encouraging children and young people to join plans to organise terrorist activities and demonstrations, or online attacks.

Teachers and schools can help to counter online extremism by exposing it as an issue that can have serious implications for all students. The aim is to bring the concern out of the dark so that pupils are aware of it and can look out for signs of it online. It is also important to offer pupils a counter-narrative to extreme views and to discuss with them some of the underlying reasons for online extremism.

Issue 6: Theft, fraud, scams and phishing
The use of digital technologies to undertake criminal deception for financial or personal gain.

A number of criminal activities take place through digital technologies with the aim of defrauding children and young people. These activities do not normally pose an immediate threat to pupils' safety, but victims of fraud can experience shorter- and longer-term mental distress.

The activities usually fall into the following three categories:

- Attempts to steal money or personal information from children and young people through direct requests.
- Attempts to get children and young people to self-infect their own computers by downloading malware that finds, and sends to the criminal, personal data from a computer, laptop or phone.
- Attempts to steal a child's or young person's identity so the criminal can commit a crime using their identity.

In a 2015 study with 19,000 respondents from 144 countries worldwide, Intel Security found that 97% of users could not identify a sophisticated phishing email. As detailed in the 2021 Data Breach Investigations report, 30% of phishing messages are opened by targeted users; of these users, 12% click on the malicious attachments or links included in the messages.

In 2019, the Commission for Countering Extremism found that 25% of the general public in the UK had witnessed extremism online. In addition, a research study with 706 members of the public found in 2020 that around 7% of participants had specifically searched for extremist content online.

A common issue for pupils is being targeted by criminals attempting to defraud them through phishing communications. Phishing is believed to have originated in around 1995, when the internet first became popular. However, it did not become a prevalent crime that could impact on school pupils' safety until around 2005. This form of online crime involves scammers sending out thousands and sometimes millions of communications, normally automatically, to try to steal other users' personal information, such as passwords, bank account numbers and addresses. Contact lists, sometimes found on the dark web, are used by those committing this crime. The availability of so-called phishing kits that provide the software required to steal users' personal information makes it a crime that people with limited tech knowledge can commit. Variants of this crime include spear phishing, which involves sophisticated attempts to target one individual, and whale phishing, which is an attempt to trick high-value targets, such as heads of companies.

Examples of the types of fraud that children and young people might be exposed to include:

- **Fake offers**: children and young people are scammed by 'too good to be true' offers, perhaps from travel companies or gaming companies promising to give away gifts or money.
- **Lottery scams**: telling children and young people they have won money and need to click through a link to claim it.
- **Hitman scams**: communications suggesting that someone knows private and personal information about a child or young person and that this information will be shared unless a ransom is paid.
- **Fake shopping**: offers on products that children and young people will like (shoes, clothes, etc.) that are not real. Money is sent and the product never arrives.

PRIVACY
The use of digital technologies to invade and exploit others' privacy.

CASE STUDY

It is often said that 'what happens online stays online'. Indeed, removing online information permanently is difficult and time-consuming, since users need to get in touch with the tech companies hosting their content and make formal requests. Even if users merely wish to delete a photo or comment from their own profiles, there is no guarantee that these have not already been shared and are circulating online. This can be hard to track.

The information that we, as users, leave behind us online – ranging from personal data and user-generated content to how many times we visit a website or for how long – is stored by tech companies and is generally referred to as our 'digital footprint'. Unfortunately, children and young people are often unaware of the existence and the implications of their digital footprints, especially in terms of the repercussions these may have on their lives, jobs and futures.

These repercussions are well exemplified by the cases of celebrities and public servants in the UK who have posted controversial content online when they were young and have paid the price later, in ways that have impacted on their reputations and careers. Take the case of Paris Brown, appointed in 2013 as the UK's first youth police and crime commissioner. The 17-year-old's position did not last long: she resigned after public criticism of – and an investigation into – inappropriate tweets that she had posted when she was 14, considered by many to be racist and homophobic. Similarly, the British cricketer Ollie Robinson received an eight-match ban in 2021 because of sexist comments he had made online between 2012 and 2014, when he was aged 18-20.

When Brown and Robinson's comments came back to haunt them years later, it was too late. They both apologised, but the language they had used – which they never imagined would one day resurface – had a negative impact on their reputations and careers.

Both cases suggest that, as children and young people spend a large part of their day using social media platforms, it is essential that they are educated about how to use these platforms in ways that are not just virtuous and mindful of the language they use, but also underpinned by an awareness of the possible consequences of their online actions. Through personal development time, tutor time or PSHE lessons, pupils need to be taught how to manage their privacy settings, what risks are involved in giving information away to the platforms they use, and ultimately to be reflective about the possible long-term consequences of what they do online.

Privacy invasion is a threat to children's and young people's safety. Some pupils might see giving up personal information to internet corporations and social media platforms as not a threat at all, or worth it for their access to free software and the benefits it brings to them. However, it is important that pupils learn how their data is used, as the information that tech companies hold about them will affect the rest of their lives. It is essential that pupils also understand the implications of leaving information and data behind, and the repercussions this may have in the future.

This is why, when it comes to the risks presented by digital technologies in terms of privacy, the main threats faced by children and young people are data-tracking – which refers to the collection, monitoring and profiling of their data by tech companies – and the extent to which their digital interactions today become their digital footprint, which can have an adverse impact later in life.

Issue 7: Data-tracking
The process of collecting, storing and profiling users' personal information and content online, for the purposes of commodification, advertising and/or monitoring.

Anyone who has watched Netflix's documentary *The Social Dilemma* will be well aware of the issues faced by our societies in terms of data-tracking. There are many terms that describe the process of individuals or organisations collecting personal data online, including data analytics, data collection, data-mining, data-warehousing, data-harvesting, data-scraping and the more overarching term that we use here, data-tracking. The reason why most websites and online platforms used by children and young people are free of charge is that those running the websites and platforms make money by collecting users' data. As the saying goes, it is internet users who are the product. That is, users' data, from their personal information to their user-generated content, is sold by tech companies to advertising firms and other interested parties.

Given the power of digital technologies and advances in data storage, companies can collect every piece of information given away by users (what they like, what they look at, for how long, when, etc.) and hold personal profiles on all their users. In many cases, this data is used for reasons that may be fairly harmless, such as targeted commercial advertising. However, it could also be put to more malicious use, ranging from voter manipulation to the influencing of political opinions, based on invasions of personal privacy, profiling and targeted political advertising. You may remember the Cambridge Analytica scandal, where personal information was taken without authorisation in the 2010s to build a system that could profile individual US voters, with a view to targeting them with personalised political advertisements capitalising on their worries and concerns. The data of around 50 million Facebook users was harvested by Cambridge Analytica.

In 2018, Ofcom found that 58% of adult internet users in the UK had concerns about how their data is used and about their privacy.

It is therefore essential that children and young people are encouraged to understand that nothing is private on the internet, and that what they like, post or share becomes the property of tech companies (even when users delete their own personal information or user-generated content). Relatedly, pupils need to know that their data is subject to constant processes of commodification, profiling and monitoring.

To help pupils think about what data might be tracked and what internet corporations might know about them, teachers could ask them to complete the following table. Pupils may be asked to add two or more tech companies that they use at the bottom of the table.

Company	What might this company know about me
Google	
TikTok	
Netflix	
Amazon	
Snapchat	
Instagram	

Issue 8: Digital footprint

Information, which can be used for good or bad ends, left behind by users on the internet as a result of their online activity.

> According to a survey conducted by CareerBuilder, an employment website with offices across the world, 70% of employers say they screen potential employees on social media and that what they find affects hiring decisions.

Pupils need to learn that every time they post something on social media, visit a website or post a video, this leaves a digital footprint. All their interactions are being stored as data and, once combined, these interactions become their digital legacies. What children and young people post online can come back to haunt them at any time. It can be seen by future employers, partners or even their own children. Pupils should understand that their digital legacies can be good or bad, since they provide evidence about the best and worst of themselves.

There are two forms of digital footprint:

- **Active footprint**: all the content, photos and data that pupils post online and are collected.
- **Passive footprint**: the data collected without users' knowledge, such as how many times they visit a website and for how long.

These forms of digital footprint are closely related to the problem of data-tracking and to how tech companies operate and run their businesses. Not only do internet corporations and social media platforms engage in practices of data collection for commercial purposes, but the ways in which the digital environment is designed make it hard for users to take ownership and control of the information they post, share and create. Implemented in 2018, the General Data Protection Regulation (GDPR) is a piece of EU data-protection legislation intended to give users more control over their data. Companies are now expected to prioritise users' privacy by design, to seek informed consent before collecting their data, and to give users the right to request that companies erase their personal data (this is known as the 'right to be forgotten'). Even though the UK has left the EU, the UK government has issued an amendment that aligns its original laws on data protection with the requirements of GDPR, thus creating a new data protection framework known as 'UK GDPR'.

Even though GDPR is a step towards better protecting users' privacy in the digital age, the job of clearing one's own digital footprint from the internet is still difficult and time-consuming. To delete something permanently from a specific platform, users need to get in touch with the tech company that runs the platform. This, however, does not resolve the problem of posts, photos and videos being potentially shared with others before any sensitive content is removed. Relatedly, if the aim is not necessarily to delete something permanently, but for others not to see content that might come back to haunt users, then children and young people need to become more digitally savvy and to better understand the privacy implications of engaging with digital technologies.

Indeed, a key problem is that the internet was not designed for, nor does it take into account, the maturity levels of younger users. It is natural for children and young people to experiment, make mistakes and live in the moment. In the most part, this is because they have not had time to learn about the consequences of their actions. In fact, children often learn about consequences through making mistakes. If they get their fingers burnt after posting on social media something they think is funny, many will be less likely to do it again. The problem, however, is that what children and young people write and post online is often preserved or shared in ways that are difficult to track and erase, thus becoming their permanent digital footprint. The internet never forgets.

The first step in helping children and young people to maintain a clean and positive digital legacy is to encourage them to look into the future. Teachers might start by sharing stories of young people whose lives have been affected by misjudged or inappropriate posts. They might ask their pupils questions such as:

- What could you do online today that you would be happy to be remembered for?
- What could you do online today that you would *not* want to be remembered for?

In doing so, teachers can help pupils to learn about privacy online and about how to manage their own privacy. This will involve showing pupils how to manage privacy settings in popular apps: almost all apps that involve some form of interaction have privacy settings, where pupils can choose how much data they wish to share with others and with the companies that make the apps. Finally, teachers need to help pupils think about who they want to be. Teachers have a responsibility to project a positive image by offering exemplars and, among other things, inspiration and guidance.

MISTRUST
The use of digital technologies to increase mistrust in society.

Trust is a major issue for many users of digital technologies, who are concerned about who and what they can trust online – and for good reason.[84] With the rise of misinformation and so-called fake news, plus the fact that people may not represent themselves truthfully online, children and young people are likely to encounter a great deal of content as they grow up that makes them question what they can and cannot believe online. It is important that pupils are taught to be watchful and wary about issues relating to trust online, but there is a delicate balance to be struck here: they should not become scared or paranoid to the extent of losing all trust in people or institutions.

Indeed, the problem of mistrust relates to whether or not we can trust individual users online and, more problematically, to whether or not we can trust institutions, including the media, the sociopolitical system and experts. As such, the main issues that are currently associated with mistrust and may affect children and young people are misinformation, the construction of distorted identities and plagiarism. These issues may lead to children and young people either being subjected to mistruths or not being truthful and trustworthy in their own actions online. Some of these actions will have few or no consequences, while others will affect the wellbeing of pupils and other people. Unfortunately, the greater the amount of mistrust mediated through digital technologies, the greater the amount the mistrust within our societies. This can have negative repercussions on the credibility of individuals, organisations, institutions and, ultimately, democracy.

Issue 9: Misinformation
False or inaccurate information that is mediated through digital technologies and may be deliberately designed to deceive.

CASE STUDY

A simple piece of A4 paper might seem an unlikely prop to manipulate children into dangerous eating habits, but that is exactly what it became in one online craze. The trend, known as the A4 waist challenge, started in China and went viral in 2016. It encouraged posing before a mirror with a piece of A4 paper in front of your torso – if you were wider than the paper, you were classed as 'fat'. This is nonsense, of course. But not, sadly, to the impressionable young children who accepted it as fact and went on to starve themselves in a bid to slim down to the size of a sheet of paper.

This is just one example of many trends and challenges that start online but take hold in schools at an alarming pace. These trends, which children can easily access online, gain popularity in ways that are often unnoticed by adults, many of whom are unaware of how easily misinformation can spread through seemingly harmless sites.

Balancing curiosity with rational scepticism is a skill we all need to learn – and never more so than in the digital age, when so many manipulative and potentially dangerous claims are readily available at the click of a button. As misinformation becomes more prevalent, it is becoming harder and harder for users, especially younger ones, to distinguish truth from fiction. In an online world where nothing is certain, children and young people need to gain the confidence to constructively question what they are presented with, rather than believe everything they are told or see on screen.

From low-level mistruths regarding friendships and childhood conversations to potentially more dangerous trends such as the A4 waist challenge, rumours and other upsetting and harmful information have been known to spill into the classroom, affecting friendships, behaviour and learning. During the Covid-19 pandemic, for instance, many mistruths were spread, with social media platforms serving as a main vehicle and a main culprit, since they use algorithms that make information visible depending on its popularity and not its reliability.

As one Year 6 teacher in a Manchester primary school told us, many conspiracy theories circulated during the pandemic that seemed to exacerbate anxieties among parents and children. As a result, the school's trust published a booklet written with the Visual Social Media Lab at Manchester Metropolitan University to support staff and parents in identifying possible mistruths. The booklet was shared with the whole school community and with other schools across Manchester, in order to highlight the prevalence of fake news and encourage people to more readily question what they were reading. Meanwhile, school leaders aimed to ensure good and constant communication with parents and pupils by using social media platforms. Indeed, although these platforms can represent a risk in terms of the spread of misinformation, when used proactively they are beneficial in terms of disseminating messages faster and more widely.

What can we do?

It is never too early to start equipping children with the skills they need to spot misinformation online. By implementing targeted programmes, schools can encourage children from the age of three to start recognising the difference between truth and lies. Storybooks are a great way of teaching this, giving young children the opportunity to identify lies and to discuss the reasons why someone may want to manipulate facts and claims. In key stage 2 and onwards, discussing different forms of misinformation (including, for example, the manipulation of photographs) can enable pupils to appreciate the ease with which something can be distorted in ways that give it a whole new meaning.

In the classroom, teachers could use a simple checklist like the one below to promote practical steps that everyone can take in order to check whether online information is real or manipulated.

- **Check sources**. Does the story say where the information comes from? If there is no source or citation, it might not be real.
- **Reflect on the boundaries of your own knowledge**. How much do you know about the story? Ask somebody you trust and/or check accredited sources like reputable news outlets.
- **Assess the URL of the website**. Does it look reliable? Is the domain associated with official sources (as in the case of .gov, which stands for 'government')?
- **Assess the language used and the layout of the website**. Do they look reliable? Are there any typos or spelling mistakes? Is the language too sensationalist?
- **Google the story**. Compare and contrast information about the story across multiple sources that you find on Google. Are mainstream news sites reporting on the story? Or has it been debunked by official sources?
- **Look beyond the first results on Google**. Results on Google are organised according to the popularity of websites and what you have liked and browsed before, so check beyond the first results and use Google alongside other search engines like DuckDuckGo.
- **Use the Google reverse image search function**. You can use this function to try to find out the origin of the image or if it has been used before; this may help you to debunk questionable online

content. As well as Google's reverse image search function, you could use sites like tineye.com.

- **Use fact-checking websites**. Organisations dedicated to fact-checking information can be helpful, so check to see if the story has been debunked on sites like fullfact.org.

- **Diversify your exposure to information**. Social media platforms like Facebook and Twitter use algorithms that expose users to information that aligns with their own pre-existing views and opinions. Make the conscious effort to deliberately follow individuals and organisations with opposing views to yours. This will expose you to a wider range of information, which can help you to better spot misinformation.

- **Think before sharing**. Does the story sound real? Could it cause harm if you share it? Are your own beliefs influencing your judgement? How does the story make you feel? Often, misinformation is designed to make people angry or upset so they share it.

This list is adapted from Gianfranco Polizzi's tips on how to evaluate online content and the booklet *Stop. Think. Share? A Teacher's Guide to Mis- and Disinformation During the Covid-19 Pandemic*, developed by the Wise Owl Trust and the Visual Social Media Lab at Manchester Metropolitan University.

A survey conducted in 2019 by Google found that 45% of the British public believe they encounter fake news online every day.

The term 'misinformation' refers to false or inaccurate information, and when this is produced with the purpose of intentionally causing harm it is generally referred to as 'disinformation'. The term 'fake news' describes the misrepresentation of facts and events, and the invention of stories that can serve to deceive and manipulate others. Although the telling of untruths has always been part of the human condition, the invention of the internet has amplified the extent to which lies may be spread, not just between individuals and among small groups but globally. One of the main drivers of the fake news phenomenon online is profit: these untrue yet sensational stories have the potential to attract large audiences and advertising clicks. Of course, there are many other motivations for spreading misinformation online:

- Creating a culture of suspicion and mistrust of experts and facts.
- Spreading fear and anxiety.
- Spreading conspiracy theories.
- Manipulation.
- Influencing democratic debate.
- Promoting an ideology.
- Getting revenge.
- Jealousy.

Pupils have always made stories up about other pupils – this is not new. The internet, however, has accelerated the extent to which this can happen and brought a wider audience to these stories. As a result, teachers face the challenge of trying to understand what the increasing spread of misinformation online is doing their pupils' sense of right and wrong. If misinformation is seen by pupils to be normal and expected, this will likely make them more cynical and suspicious. As a result, it is important for pupils to understand that people who do not hold a regard for speaking the truth may lack both honesty and integrity.

> In the first quarter of 2018, Facebook reported removing 583 million fake accounts.

Schools have a role in helping their pupils to think about whether they are deliberately posting mistruths online – and if so, why. At the same time, schools need to help pupils become critical users of digital technologies and online content. Pupils cannot take everything they see or read at face value; they have to learn to ask questions and challenge what they read on their timelines and newsfeeds. This puts teachers in a difficult position. We should not expect pupils to leave lessons feeling fearful and not believing anything to be 'true', but at the same time they need to be realistic about the nature of modern communication. It is easy to spread misinformation online and there are powerful economic, political, social and other incentives for doing so.

In 2017, Ofcom found that more than half (54%) of 12- to 15-year-olds in the UK used social media platforms such as Facebook and Twitter to access online news, making social media the second most popular source of news after television (62%). Nearly three-quarters (73%) of teens were aware of the concept of fake news and four in 10 (39%) said they had seen a fake news story online or on social media platforms.

Teachers can start by encouraging pupils to look at and critically evaluate their own digitally mediated communications. They can ask questions such as: do you strongly believe that what you are about to post is true? What is the evidence base for what you are writing? Should you post something if you are not sure of its factual basis? What will be the consequences of not posting it?

Issue 10: Distorted identities
Identities that are not representative of the truth and are crafted by children and young people themselves using digital technologies.

The internet provides children with a powerful tool to craft their identities – a tool that can maintain or undermine their integrity and how other people see them. Given that social media platforms encourage popularity based on attracting followers and friends, and given that peer pressure is a common concern when growing up, it is perhaps not surprising how keen children and young people are to display the best sides of themselves. Digital technologies enable pupils to present themselves in ways that allow them to gain greater peer affirmation. These technologies provide a new stage on which pupils can act as performers who craft and present their identities.[85]

The distinguished Harvard academic Howard Gardner and his co-author Katie Davis have called this the 'packaged self'.[86] They say the desire of young people to package themselves online is driven by three interconnected Is: identity, intimacy and imagination. Their argument is that young people seek to present themselves online in certain ways and as if they are involved in a form of public performance. This is undertaken in order to drive intimacy with others – intimacy that is forged, documented, controlled and sustained through the tools provided by social media platforms. What is important here is imagination: the ability to express oneself creatively to gain attention. Although, in most cases, Gardner, Davis and others who have written on this topic think such actions are largely harmless, they do raise some ethical questions linked to truth and authenticity.

A survey carried out by Photoion Photography School in 2015 found that nearly 70% of internet users edit their selfies before posting them. This includes men and women.

In 2017, the most popular paid app on Apple's App Store was Facetune, a selfie-editing app that allows users to 'photoshop' their photos before posting them. Children and young people often use the app to produce retouched images of themselves (they can whiten their teeth, narrow their waist, remove a spot, etc.). It has also become reasonably common for them to use filters on Instagram. Indeed, considering the popularity of the selfie, named the word of the year by Oxford Dictionaries in 2013,[87] it is not surprising how popular Facetune and filters have become. However, this raises the question of whether digital technologies play a role not just in crafting children's and young people's identities, but also – when used excessively in ways underpinned by feelings of insecurity and low self-esteem – in somehow distorting or even fabricating their identities.

This is why teachers have a moral duty to help pupils question their actions and motivations to distort their identities online. Questions for discussion may include: how much are you willing to distort 'true' representations of yourselves to attract followers? Will your integrity be questioned if you use features of social media platforms to augment those parts of yourselves that you like and downplay the ones you are less keen on? Of course, we all do this in some form or another, online and offline. However, pupils today have access to much more powerful tools that allow them to not only enhance but also distort their identities in ways that are not true to who they are. If they push the limits too far, their authenticity as well as their integrity will be called into question.

Issue 11: Plagiarism
Taking others' ideas from online sources and passing them off as one's own.

> In 2012, a seven-year study with more than 70,000 high school pupils in the US found that 58% had plagiarised content.[88]

Plagiarism carried out through digital technologies has been a growing concern for schools since the turn of the century. Although plagiarism might not be viewed as a crime by many, as there are often no direct victims, copying and pasting others' ideas and content is unethical and symptomatic of behaviour that is untruthful and untrustworthy, which is why it is included here as a risk associated with mistrust. When such behaviour infringes copyright rules, plagiarism can become illegal. Most plagiarism in schools is an issue of intellectual or academic integrity – pupils not being honest about the source of their work.

It is becoming increasingly common for pupils to use Google or other search engines to do their homework, often copying and pasting whole sections of Wikipedia. Although this might not be viewed as plagiarism *per se* if the source of the idea is not acknowledged, this counts as plagiarism under our definition: taking others' ideas from online sources and passing them off as one's own. Plagiarism becomes much more serious when it relates to assessment, such as copied essays and other forms of assignment.

> Figures compiled by *The Guardian* in 2018 show that cases of academic misconduct at Russell Group universities in the UK surged by 40% between 2014-15 and 2016-17, from 2,640 to 3,721.

Schools should encourage pupils to be courageous and diligent in order to come up with and express their own ideas. Teachers might seek to reward these qualities and the resulting creativity when they mark pupils' work. They should also explain that plagiarism at university level is a serious offence that may result in students being removed from courses. Schools can use technological solutions to try to tackle plagiarism, such as software and programs that check work for its originality. While universities spend a great deal of time and money seeking to educate students about why they should not plagiarise and trying to catch them if they do, the issue is taken less seriously in most schools. However, if pupils learn to get away with plagiarism in school they are more likely to think they can get away with it at university, where the consequences will be more serious.

WELLBEING
The use of digital technologies in a way that reduces the mental and/or physical wellbeing of users.

CASE STUDY

In secondary education, the number of pupils who use social media platforms such as Instagram, TikTok and Facebook has surged. Teachers have also witnessed a sharp increase in online incidents and concerns around digital wellbeing, since pupils were kept indoors and thrust online while we weathered the storm of the Covid-19 pandemic. One by-product of the increased use of social media is young people's need for constant reassurance around body image through 'likes' or 'reactions' on these platforms.

During a PSHE lesson at a secondary school in Greater Manchester, a class explored the impact of social media on wellbeing and mental health. During the class discussion, one Year 10 pupil was brave enough to share some of the realities she was experiencing linked to social media. The pupil said that when she uploads a picture to her Instagram account, she constantly monitors the likes she receives. She repeatedly picks up her phone to check the post and this prevents her from sleeping if she uploads a picture later in the evening.

The pupil added that if the post does not reach a certain number of likes, she will remove it as she worries about what people will think. She will then start to question how she looks and her own body image, becoming extremely anxious. In summary, the pupil uses the number of likes as a metric of her own self-worth and appearance, which is problematic. When the teacher explored this issue a little further through the class discussion, the pupil mentioned that a number of her friends and people in the same year group also viewed and used likes in this way; there was a general consensus from the class on this point.

What can be done?

To help pupils explore this sensitive topic, a hypothetical moral dilemma could be created and shared with pupils in a safe environment, such as tutor time, PSHE or personal development lessons. Ground rules need to be established first to create a culture of respect and compassion when discussing sensitive topics.

Teachers could present the following hypothetical moral dilemma:

> *You post a selfie on your Instagram account and get zero likes in 24 hours.*

- *What would you do, if anything at all?*
- *What emotions might you feel or experience?*
- *Why do likes matter to you? What do they show? Are they really important?*
- *If this happened to one of your friends, what advice would you give them?*

The teacher could use the structured talk prompts below to facilitate class discussion.

In this book, we use 'digital wellbeing' as a broad term to describe the effect of digital technologies on the mental and/or physical health of users. 'Wellbeing' is also linked to happiness and to how users subjectively feel about their lives, and may be closely related to the concept of digital flourishing. Digital flourishing is not about hedonistic pleasure or simply having fun; it refers to something more authentic, deep and sustaining. It is the sense of wellbeing, harmony and genuine happiness that we experience when we feel we are contributing positively to the digital world and our interactions bring positive benefits to our health and happiness and those of others.

A great deal of attention is paid in news articles and reports from government and other institutions to the negative influence of digital technologies on the wellbeing of children and young people. It is important to say here that much of the research behind some of these claims is disputed and there is no clear evidence of the exact effects of digital technologies on children's and young people's wellbeing. There is, however, some evidence to show that pupils' use of digital technologies can have negative consequences, including too much screen time, increased risk of self-harm and exposure to inappropriate content. It is also important to stress that the impact of these technologies on wellbeing is not necessarily negative.[89] Such technologies can improve pupils' wellbeing and there is a growing market of apps that claim to help children lead happier, healthier and more active lives.

It is important that teachers take a balanced view about wellbeing to counter commentators who have suggested that digital technologies might end up being responsible for the destruction of childhood. More sober arguments about the negative effects of these technologies have, however, been made by reputable sources. Here are three examples:

- In 2017-18, the Millennium Cohort Study based on 14-year-olds' reporting of their emotional problems found that 24% of girls and 9% of boys suffered from depression. Links to the internet were made throughout the report.[90]
- In 2019, the UK's chief medical officers recommended a precautionary approach to managing children's exposure to digital technologies. A systematic map of reviews showed a potential link between screen time and mental health issues including anxiety and depression.[91]
- In 2021, researchers at Harvard University found that users of popular social media apps like Snapchat, Facebook and TikTok were more likely to score high on a depression scale. As the research team concluded, 'Social media use was associated with greater likelihood of subsequent increase in depressive symptoms after adjustment for sociodemographic features and news sources.

These data cannot elucidate the nature of this association but suggest the need for further study.'[92]

Issue 12: Screen time
The amount of time that digital devices such as smartphones, laptops, gaming machines and televisions are used.

In 2019, Ofcom found that around two-thirds of 12- to 15-year-olds in the UK (63%) considered that they ultimately achieved 'a good balance between screen time and doing other things'.

The fear that children and young people are spending too much time in front of a screen is perhaps one of the most persistent concerns of parents and teachers. The invention of gaming machines, social media and on-demand television has led to news stories and research showing that many pupils are spending most of their time out of school looking at a screen – and this includes much of the night.[93] Gaming addiction is now recognised by the World Health Organization as a medical condition.

Fears about too much screen time tend to focus on the effects on pupils' wellbeing. Concerns include:

- **Lack of sleep**: pupils are tired for lessons and screen time has a negative impact on their learning and behaviour.
- **Lack of movement**: pupils are not moving around. This has a negative effect on their physical health, which can lead to increasing obesity levels, as well as on their mental health, which may be linked to depression and anxiety.
- **Lack of balance**: pupils are 'missing out' on learning and other opportunities as they spend too much time in front of the screen.
- **Lack of face-to-face interaction**: what has been referred to as being 'alone together'.[94]

According to Ofcom, 71% of UK children aged 12-15 in 2018 were allowed to take their mobile phone to bed.

It is important to note that screen time in and of itself is not necessarily problematic, and that what matters most is the quality of children's and young people's use of the internet, not the quantity. Most teachers would be pleased if their pupils were to spend an hour or two after school each day doing their homework on their laptops and researching online sources. Spending time using digital technologies can be beneficial for homework and for learning in general. It is also the best way to find out how these technologies work, making it easier to learn about coding, AI and other areas that will be important to pupils' lives in the future.

Teachers, therefore, should not adopt an outright negative stance on screen time, but instead be more nuanced and consider the effects relating to individual pupils' lives. The key questions are how pupils use screens, what they use them for and when they use them. There are specific concerns about the content accessed during screen time, which we will unpack below in the context of the other issues linked to wellbeing.

Issue 13: Inappropriate content
Content found on-screen that is deemed inappropriate for pupils of different ages and developmental stages.

Recently, Ofsted's chief inspector of schools, Amanda Spielman, commented that the television watershed is meaningless because of YouTube.[95] The rules governing what can be shown on television before the watershed of 9pm were designed to protect young people from accessing inappropriate content. However, pupils can now access such content online at any time. A report from Ofcom in 2021 makes clear that the communications regulator feels tech companies themselves have to do more. The report shows that 70% of users of video-sharing platforms have been exposed to a potential online harm and provides guidance on how video-sharing websites and apps in the UK could better protect their users, especially teenagers.[96] Dame Melanie Dawes, Ofcom's chief executive, said: 'Online videos play a huge role in our lives now, particularly for children. But many people see hateful, violent or inappropriate material while using them.'[97]

Whether it is seen as a responsibility for teachers, parents, tech companies, policymakers or pupils themselves, there is a concern that exposure to inappropriate content could harm children and young people. Of greatest concern is violent content and pornography that can accessed online. Exposure to violence and pornography is a perennial concern for parents

– one that has been exacerbated by digital technologies. Promisingly, there is a long history of research that has explored whether there is a correlation between pornography and violence.[98] However, there are no conclusive findings as to the impact of pornography on children, which is partly due to a paucity of quality research in this area.

Concerns about underage access to pornographic content mainly surround the following themes:

- Unrealistic expectations about what sex is, resulting in pressure for pupils to act in certain ways.
- Pornography undermining sexual consent, and changing values and beliefs about relationships.
- Issues linked to addiction to online pornography.
- Changing expectations in adult relationships – pupils do not understand what is 'normal'.
- Increased sexual violence and harassment between pupils.
- Pornography that is characterised by themes of aggression, power and control can blur the line between pleasure and violence.

Meanwhile, concerns about underage access to violence through digital technologies mainly surround these themes:

- Pupils develop the view that the world is more dangerous than it is, which could increase the chance that a child will act aggressively.
- Pupils are desensitised to the pain and suffering of others.
- Those exposed to violence become more antisocial and emotionally distressed.

Issue 14: Depression and self-harm
A mental health condition linked to feelings of sadness that can lead to self-harm.

Data analysed for BBC Radio 4 in 2021 showed that the number of children aged 9-12 admitted to hospital having hurt themselves intentionally had risen in the UK from 221 in 2013-14 to 508 in 2019-20.

Research shows that children and young people are increasingly self-reporting that digital technologies are having a negative impact on their depression and that this is leading some to self-harm. The issue is primarily linked to negative feelings about appearance and body image. Studies have shown that girls are more likely to find fault with their appearance and go on to suffer a greater number of depressive episodes.[99] The concern is that the use of social media platforms creates idealised body images that are impossible to live up to.

DIGITAL OPPORTUNITIES

In this section, we provide an overview of five areas in which digital technologies present opportunities for pupils (see the table below) and include case studies of how these opportunities manifest.

Opportunity	Definition
Learning	The use of digital technologies to enhance learning.
Connection	The use of digital technologies to make new connections and develop constructive relationships.
Leisure	The use of digital technologies to express creativity and pursue opportunities of leisure and entertainment.
Employment	The use of digital technologies to further employment and career opportunities.
Citizenship	The use of digital technologies to enhance democratic and civic participation.

LEARNING
The use of digital technologies to enhance learning.

CASE STUDY

When the Covid-19 pandemic hit the world and schools were forced to close their gates to pupils in March 2020, the use of digital technologies to deliver education boomed. Overnight, schools and educators had to digitalise their curricula and pedagogy, and many lessons were learned as the primary and secondary education sector entered uncharted water. Teachers had to explore, test and implement new teaching strategies in order to deliver lessons through a screen.

This was a huge test for teachers and some worried that their teacher pedagogy, which they had honed over multiple years in the classroom, was now defunct. Evidence and books like Doug Lemov's *Teaching in the Online Classroom*[100] provided teachers with an insight into 'best bets' in terms of practice. While this shift online was seismic for some practitioners, teachers across the UK, as in other countries, took it in their stride and did the best they could to deliver purposeful education to their pupils in challenging circumstances.

When talking about how digital technologies can enhance leaning, it would be foolish not to first mention how teachers were able to deliver, with the use of platforms such as Zoom and Microsoft Teams, synchronous (live) and asynchronous (pre-recorded) lessons and to broadcast these into the homes of children. The use of these platforms meant that subject experts who knew their pupils well could still deliver content and impart essential knowledge to their classes.

At this difficult time, teachers and form tutors were able to connect with harder-to-reach families and/or communities because platforms like Zoom or Teams were more accessible. In addition, digital parents' evenings and welfare checks become widespread practice, and some of these strategies were continued once lockdown restrictions were lifted.

During this time, we saw the creation of organisations such as Oak National Academy (www.thenational.academy), which provides an online classroom and resource hub for teachers in the UK, and huge developments in the learning platform Seneca Learning (www.senecalearning.com). These platforms allow pupils to access pre-prepared and high-quality curriculum resources from their own homes and personal devices. Now that the education sector in the UK has returned to face-to-face teaching and the school gates have reopened, many teachers are still using these two platforms to provide 'flipped learning' to their pupils to support what goes on in the classroom. Practitioners now have a wealth of resources to tap into and pupils can be redirected in ways that extend their learning beyond the classroom.

Before the Covid-19 pandemic, e-learning was becoming increasingly popular – now it is booming. Some have argued that learning enhanced through digital technologies is a sustaining innovation that does not revolutionise but largely extends what is already offered. However, if e-learning succeeds in replacing rather than supplementing face-to-face courses, it might become a disruptive innovation. As we write this book during the pandemic, it is not quite clear whether the education sector as a whole will entirely get back to what it was before – i.e. mainly classroom-based and face to face.

The Covid-19 pandemic resulted in schools shutting across the world. As reported by the World Economic Forum, more than 1.2 billion children globally were out of the classroom during the pandemic, with many learning online when digital technologies were available.

The initial sign of a move towards e-learning was the rise of the massive open online course (MOOC) in 2011, when some professors at Stanford University put their courses online and made them available to anyone who wanted to take them. The attractions of learning online were obvious: great content could be made available to anyone with an internet connection and could be accessed at any time. In the past 10 years, universities have increasingly moved their courses online, and many schools now complement in-class lessons with online homework and extended learning opportunities. Learning, for many, has become hybrid. As technology improves education, the latter is likely to be increasingly dominated by technologies, with some even predicting robot teachers.

As reported by the accountancy firm KPMG and IMD Business School, in 1995 just 4% of corporations across the world used online learning. Today, 90% of organisations use some form of e-learning in their training.

In this book, we use the term 'e-learning' to mean any form of education that at least partly utilises the internet. We employ it as an umbrella term that encompasses synchronous and asynchronous forms of online learning, digital learning, distance learning, technology-enhanced learning and other similar types of learning.

The digitalisation of learning has many perceived benefits, primarily:

- **Flexibility**: learners can learn at any time and in any place (if asynchronous).
- **Independent learning**: a greater onus is placed on learners to access learning.
- **Access to learning from experts** located around the world.
- **Enhanced technical skills**.
- **Efficiency**: pupils spend time learning while not having to physically travel to places of learning.
- **Affordability**: it is argued (although this is disputed) that e-learning is cheaper than face-to-face learning.
- **Individualised**: more personalised learning routes can be taken to suit different learning styles and approaches.

At the same time, there are several perceived disadvantages of e-learning, including:

- **Technology**: learning depends on access to working technologies, hardware, software and the internet.
- **More screen time**: learners lose the interaction that comes with meeting and learning face to face with others and in more dynamic classrooms.
- **Isolation**: learners often learn on their own. Even when they are in video conferences and discussion boards, they are normally alone.
- **Formality**: lessons online often feel more informal and some of the interactivity and spontaneity that comes from learning in the same space with others can be lost.
- **Teacher quality**: it takes different skills to teach online rather than face to face, and there are few professional development opportunities for those who teach online, which may affect the quality of learning.

Despite these challenges, e-learning is here to stay and is likely to become an increasing part of pupils' lives. Universities are moving more of their courses to online platforms as students like the flexibility of e-learning. Professional learning is also going online to suit workers and enable them to fit learning around their day jobs. Schools need to teach pupils how best to learn online and ensure they maximise the opportunities that come with e-learning. This includes working on the character qualities required to be successful when learning online, including motivation, perseverance and independent thought.

CONNECTION
The use of digital technologies to make new connections and develop constructive relationships.

CASE STUDY

As part of the Flourishing Life Leaders student leadership programme, implemented in 2021 at St Mary's Catholic High School in Wigan, Manchester, pupils were able to develop constructive relationships through the use of digital technologies. An email group was set up that included all members of the programme, drawn from Years 11-13. This simple strategy created a professional platform where pupils could engage in a dialogue around the initiatives they wished to pursue through the programme. Two members of staff were added to the group to act as the gatekeepers of ideas and to regulate the dialogue.

This form of digital communication helped to foster a sense of community among pupils and supported them to pursue common goals. Pupils also commented that they found it a useful way to keep track of the wellbeing of others in the group. For example, if a member of the team did not respond to the group emails, this acted as a flag to others and they would physically check in to see if their peer was OK and not overburdened with work or stress. The use of email, rather than a WhatsApp group, encouraged more professional dialogue between pupils, which is advantageous as they move towards the age of employment. Finally, the etiquette of the email correspondence was explicitly taught to pupils before the group was created.

According to Internet World Stats, in 2021 around 5.1 billion people were active users of the internet worldwide. This means that around 65% of the world population is online.

Perhaps more than anything else, digital technologies have revolutionised how we communicate with each other. The invention of the internet and the apps that rely on it have accelerated the extent to which individuals are able to communicate with more people, on a wider scale, more instantaneously. The internet has built on the printing press, telephone, radio and television, among other technologies, to help us communicate our thoughts, feelings and ideas with others. With the exception of the telephone, these earlier technologies required gatekeepers – people in charge of what was published or broadcast. Now, with just a Wi-Fi connection, anyone can publish or broadcast to large audiences. This presents many challenges, as exemplified by the risks we have discussed. At the same time, it provides many opportunities for pupils now and in the future.

Importantly, one of these opportunities relates to the fact that digital technologies offer children and young people a chance to build meaningful, constructive relationships not just with those around them but also much further afield. For example, children and young people can now:

- Play online games with children who live as far away as the US, India or Kenya. This helps to build connections and an understanding of different cultures.
- Connect with other children who have similar interests – this is especially positive if these interests are prosocial.
- Build communities and alliances around issues that matter – e.g. campaigning for constructive causes of social change.
- Communicate with potential employers around the world, which can lead to new adventures and opportunities for employment.

Communication in the digital age is only a good opportunity for children and young people when it is pursued responsibly and with character and wisdom. In good hands, the ability to build networks and connections at a scale that was previously impossible can bring about global change:

exemplars such as Greta Thunberg and Marcus Rashford have used social media to make a real difference. Children are growing up in a world of 'influencers' who use digital technologies to communicate to their followers; if these influencers have a positive message to send, this can be a good thing. However, communication works two ways, and it is important that pupils understand they can use their voice critically and constructively to challenge influencers if necessary.

LEISURE
The use of digital technologies to express creativity and pursue opportunities of leisure and entertainment.

CASE STUDY

A project called Engaging Libraries, funded by Wellcome Trust, was launched in 2017 in the UK with the aim of supporting public libraries to run public engagement activities. As one of its goals, the project sought to better promote digital literacy among children aged 8-12 through the development of an online game by Sutton Council Cultural Services.

The game, called *NewsFlash!*, was designed to enable children to critically evaluate information in the digital age. It was deemed important that the game should be both fun and educational: children would benefit from playing the game in terms of their own development of digital literacy skills and knowledge.

NewsFlash! asks players to investigate rumours and claims as part of their chosen characters' involvement in the production of a school newspaper. Players are prompted to interview different characters, from classmates to teachers, to find out the truth. In the meantime, they are presented with short videos encouraging them to appreciate the difference between facts and opinions, as well as the risks and opportunities that using search engines like Google can present in terms of fact-checking or the spread of misinformation.

NewsFlash! is an example of how digital technologies can be designed and used in ways that allow younger users to pursue entertainment opportunities that may also benefit their development as critical users of these technologies. It was developed by a game designer in consultation with an academic and teachers, informed by focus group discussions with pupils aged 8-12 from schools in London. The game, along with a resource pack for teachers, can be found here: www.newsflashgame.org

In a UK survey conducted in 2021, the 5Rights Foundation found that as many children and young people aged 6-17 reported enjoying playing with YouTube (96%) as enjoyed playing in real life (97%).

In this book, the term 'leisure' refers to the ways in which digital technologies can be used to express creativity and pursue opportunities for entertainment. These opportunities may be primarily individualistic – for example, watching Netflix or videos on YouTube – or more collective, such as making and sharing videos on TikTok or playing online games with other players. Undoubtedly, the internet has made it possible for all users, and particularly younger ones, to cultivate new ways of engaging in leisure activities and to do so at a faster pace and on a wider scale.

Some would argue that using digital technologies for entertainment can lead to issues of depression, internet addiction, high screen time and poor wellbeing.[101] This section does not dispute the fact that these issues may well occur as a result of overusing the internet, as discussed earlier in the book. But it would be unfair not to recognise that digital technologies have the potential to contribute to wellbeing and flourishing by providing opportunities for creativity and leisure. From an individualistic point of view, use of the internet for leisure – such as watching funny videos on YouTube – contributes to positive feelings of escapism that have been linked to individual (at least short-term) happiness.[102] Similarly, whether it is performed for one's own personal satisfaction or for the experience of connecting with others, making and sharing multimedia content on online platforms – from tutorials and reviews to videos promoting different causes – is a form of creativity.[103]

Since its invention, the internet – and, in particular, what is commonly referred to as Web 2.0 – has been praised for enabling users to act as not only consumers but also producers of information. Research shows that the internet's potential for creativity is reshaping popular culture in the digital age, as well as civic engagement in prosocial issues. Think, for instance, of the ways in which young people use the internet today to produce and promote videos about migration or the environment, thus sustaining their collective engagement as part of a community and for purposes of social justice.[104]

According to the 5Rights Foundation, children and young people in the UK reported in 2021 that their experience of playing with digital products and services had been mainly diverse (86%), social (85%) and stimulating (82%).

There is growing research showing that using digital technologies for gaming enables children and young people to engage in forms of entertainment for educational purposes,[105] as exemplified by the *NewsFlash!* case study. Through interaction with other players, use of these technologies is also beneficial for social and emotional skills, which younger users could develop or consolidate online and then apply to different offline contexts.[106] In short, although digital technologies can lead to risks associated with mental health and general wellbeing, they also provide opportunities for happiness and flourishing – opportunities that may revolve around activities of leisure and entertainment but have implications that are far-reaching.[107] For these opportunities to be realised, it is essential that pupils are encouraged to develop wisdom in relation to how they use digital technologies, allowing them to maximise their opportunities and minimise their risks.

EMPLOYMENT
The use of digital technologies to further employment and career opportunities.

CASE STUDY

An example of digital technologies being used to develop employment and career opportunities for pupils occurred at St Mary's Catholic

High School in Wigan, Manchester, which implemented a three-day work experience programme for Year 10 and Year 12 pupils in June 2020, delivered through digital technologies. The school worked with a company called Young Professionals, which delivered the programme virtually in school and broadcast live sessions into classrooms. Pupils were expected to attend school for the three days of the programme, which involved several pre-set sessions. In addition, pupils were able to choose two employer-led sessions per day.

A range of employers were involved and the school specifically selected some that were linked to growth sectors of Greater Manchester to introduce a regional context. During each session, pupils were able to ask employers from the local area direct questions and receive high-quality advice about career pathways and employment opportunities. After the event, pupils were provided with the employers' email addresses so further connections could be made.

The agenda for the programme can be seen below.

DAY 1

Form time	8.30-8.55	Form time runs as normal.
Periods 1-2	8.55-10.49	Young Professionals-led session: CV writing, interview skills, communication, problem-solving and networking.
Break	10.49-11.09	
Period 3	11.09-12.07	**Choice 1**: Chartered Institute of Management Accountants; learn about roles in the finance industry. **Choice 2**: The turning point (healthcare/charity sector); healthcare isn't just doctors and nurses.
Period 4A	12.07-12.42	Year 10 lunch and Year 12 complete an independent project.
Period 4B	12.42-13.52	Year 12 lunch and Year 10 complete an independent project.

Period 5	13.52-14.50	**Choice 1**: Being an engineer is not about fixing cars; learn more about this growing sector.
		Choice 2: Learn more about opportunities in the Royal Air Force, offering a huge number of roles and apprenticeships.

DAY 2

Form time	8.30-8.55	Form time runs as normal.
Periods 1-2	8.55-10.49	Young Professionals-led session: money skills, budgeting, financial independence, managing debt and enterprise.
Break	10.49-11.09	
Period 3	11.09-12.07	**Choice 1**: Capgemini (digital and technology consultants); learn about their latest innovation project and complete a challenge.
		Choice 2: Civil service – one of the top-rated employers in England; find out what they actually do.
Period 4A	12.07-12.42	Year 10 lunch and Year 12 complete an independent project.
Period 4B	12.42-13.52	Year 12 lunch and Year 10 complete an independent project.
Period 5	13.52-14.50	**Choice 1**: Browne Jacobson, a national law firm with offices across the country.
		Choice 2: Human resources – looking after the people behind a business; how a business works.

DAY 3

Form time	8.30-8.55	Form time runs as normal.

Periods 1-2	8.55-10.49	Young Professionals-led session: workplace etiquette, online reputation, personal branding and self-awareness.
Break	10.49-11.09	
Period 3	11.09-12.07	**Choice 1**: Ernst & Young management consultants; learn how they help businesses to improve. **Choice 2**: Creative industry – photography and film-making.
Period 4A	12.07-12.42	Year 10 lunch and Year 12 complete an independent project.
Period 4B	12.42-13.52	Year 12 lunch and Year 10 complete an independent project.
Period 5	13.52-14.50	**Choice 1**: Kitchen8 – a PR and marketing company working with many well-known brands. **Choice 2**: Cyber security – jobs for the future. Could you help to prevent cyber-attacks?

It is sometimes said that we are preparing pupils for the 21st century with a 19th-century education. The argument is that we are not helping pupils to develop the knowledge, skills and competencies that will equip them for the jobs of the future. Computing, for example, is a marginalised subject in many schools and in 2017 only just over half of all schools in England offered the subject at GCSE level.[108] According to the *Disconnected?* report published in 2021 by WorldSkills UK with Enginuity and the Learning and Work Institute, the number of young people taking IT subjects at GCSE has dropped 40% since 2015, yet the demand from employers for AI, robotics and other tech skills is growing exponentially.[109] Schools may think that employers will fill this digital skills gap, but while *Disconnected?* reveals that 70% of young people in the UK expect employers to invest in teaching them digital skills on the job, only half of the employers surveyed are able to provide that training.[110] A different survey by McKinsey, the global management consultancy, found in 2020 that 87% of business leaders in countries across the world were facing, or were expecting, serious skills shortages, while 44% said young people leaving school, college or university were not 'work-ready'.[111] It is perhaps not surprising that the McKinsey research found that many pupils develop digital skills outside school,[112] which is why formal education needs to play a more active role in addressing this gap.

An interesting example of how technology is advancing ahead of education can be seen in Blackpool. In 2020, a superfast cable was installed linking Blackpool to the US. This means data can now travel from the US to Blackpool faster than from Blackpool to London. This should provide Blackpool with the opportunity to lead digital innovation in the UK and attract digital companies to set up there. However, leaders in the area believe local pupils are not being adequately prepared to work in such companies. According to leaders, the GCSE curriculum is heavily focused on coding, which puts many pupils off studying the subject – only 5% of girls in the area choose to study computing.[113]

Given that digital skills are so important to pupils' futures, why are they not being taught well in many schools, and why do pupils not want to study the subject? The answer might lie partly in the fact that there are not enough teachers qualified to teach computing. A new computing curriculum was introduced in England in 2014, yet 75% of teachers reported that they were not confident enough in delivering the new curriculum, according to BCS, the chartered institute for IT.[114] Furthermore, the development of digital skills and knowledge should not be marginalised to a single subject, but should be a core part of all subjects across the school curriculum. Pupils should be encouraged to learn about digital technologies and how they link to maths, science, English, geography, physical education and other subjects. For example, pupils should learn that 3D printing skills are not only central to art or technology, but can also be applied to the medical, fashion and film sectors, among many others.

In 2018, the accountancy firm Deloitte found that more than 75% of business executives in the UK were struggling to recruit employees with the required digital skills.

Schools have a responsibility to teach basic IT skills, which can become the gateway through which pupils can explore and use more advanced technologies. This must be undertaken in a fun and interactive way – it should be about developing apps, websites and basic robots. Pupils also need to be encouraged to better understand the links between the skills required to use digital technologies and their future jobs. The challenge, however, is not just finding more competent teachers as the digital world continues to evolve, but building enthusiastic and enquiring minds and encouraging pupils to creatively and independently learn about digital technologies in their own lives. This will help pupils to see how learning coding links to employment in the gaming industry, or how making robots can be vital to changing people's lives in medicine. Schools should think about inviting in experts from universities and businesses (or connecting to them through webinars), as well as former pupils who hold jobs related to technology. In short, schools should showcase individuals who have changed and contributed to the digital world (perhaps through virtual reality or internet developments) and provide role models for pupils to aspire to.

CITIZENSHIP
The use of digital technologies to enhance democratic and civic participation.

CASE STUDY: DEMOCRATIC PARTICIPATION

St Mary's Catholic High School in Wigan wanted to develop a student leadership model that was inclusive of all pupils and cohorts. The leadership programme was designed to engage pupils as soon as they entered the gates in Year 7 and offer a clear progression route through to Year 13. The Flourishing Life Leaders programme links closely to the school's mission statement, as illustrated on the next page, alongside the school's character virtues.

"I can do all things through Christ who strengthens me to be a safe, happy, proud, loving person who flourishes in life."

Special thanks to Mrs Calwell, AHT for personal development at St Mary's Catholic High School, for the co-production, implementation and leadership of the school's character virtues.

Implementation phase

St Mary's decided to recruit the Year 11 Flourishing Life Leaders team first and used a Google Form to allow pupils to submit their application online. The school was able to insert professional development videos into the application form in order to provide further information to pupils about the school's character virtues. This supported pupils in evidencing and writing about how they would enact the virtues.

Using digital technologies to recruit Flourishing Life Leaders

The school received more than 300 applications from pupils to become Flourishing Life Leaders. The next stage in the recruitment process was to democratically elect the Year 11 team, including a head girl, a head boy and a group of deputies. The school wished to be guided by the school community in which individuals were appointed as the senior team.

An additional round of interviews took place for the pupils who put themselves forward for the senior team; they were also asked to create a two-minute video in which they described their manifesto and explained why they should be appointed. The school created an electronic ballot paper, in which the videos were embedded, and this ballot paper was sent to pupils and parents. In total, 2,600 votes were received, after which the senior team was appointed.

CASE STUDY: CIVIC PARTICIPATION

Another case study showing how digital technologies can be used by pupils for purposes of civic participation also comes from St Mary's. Members of the senior Flourishing Life Leaders team wanted to raise funds for Cancer Research, so they organised a 5K sponsored swim and set up a page on JustGiving, an online platform used to promote and raise funds for charitable work. Pupils publicised their page via the school's social media accounts, emails to parents and the school's own digital homework platform. In short, pupils used their digital prowess to call the community to action. Ultimately, they raised more than £1,000 for charity.

The internet has been praised by some for its potential to encourage children and young people to participate more, civically and politically. While the civic and the political are terms that overlap significantly, civic participation can be broadly understood as involvement in one's own community, which may include forms of participation such as volunteering and doing charitable work. By contrast, political participation is more concerned with affecting decision-making processes (e.g. through voting, lobbying and protesting), which is why, in the context of governance and democracy, it overlaps with the concept of democratic participation. The internet has the potential to facilitate both civic and democratic participation, as championed by many commentators.[115] Relatedly, it has been heralded by many as a means to increase levels of digital citizenship, understood here as the active use of digital technologies to participate in social and political activities guided by a sense of civic responsibility.

In a 2014 survey conducted by the think-tank Demos, 38% of young people in the UK said they had signed a petition online, 29% had used Facebook or Twitter to raise awareness of a cause, and 21% had 'liked' a political cause or group that they agreed with.

The internet has opened up new opportunities for children and young people to participate in formal and more informal decision-making processes, from joining political parties and sharing governance at school to taking part in protest events, as well as in their own communities. Terms such as 'e-citizen', 'cyber-citizen' and 'cyber-citizen 2.0' have been coined to describe this phenomenon. Digital technologies, and primarily the internet, have provided a vehicle for pupils to connect with compassionate and political causes on a local, national or global scale, and to make a difference to others, which some have argued has led them to become more socially conscious. When used for positive purposes, the internet has the potential to help pupils develop stronger connections with others and with communities more generally, and can enable them to appreciate the importance of civic ties as well as their own obligations to their communities.

Democratic participation

Democracy is increasingly moving online, formally and informally. Formally, there have been discussions in the UK and elsewhere about e-voting, although there are concerns about votes potentially being compromised, and about gaps in access to technology and digital skills that make it harder for certain groups to vote online.[116] When it comes to informal politics, civil society organisations (including, for instance, advocacy and pressure groups) and political consulting firms are increasingly using social media and other platforms to mobilise action and influence voters. This, however, comes with security risks – think of the Cambridge Analytica scandal (see page 139) – while reinforcing the problem of 'clicktivism', the idea that the internet enables users to show support easily in ways that are less likely to lead to real social change.

In terms of how children and young people can use digital technologies for democratic participation, the internet can be a great way for them to access and research different viewpoints, learn about the policies of different political parties, and join protest and campaigning groups. Of course, pupils need to develop digital literacy and become social media-savvy in order to be able to question the different positions and viewpoints they are exposed to online. At the same time, the internet is a great way for pupils to express their own views and to contact and engage with people in power. It can bring them greater efficacy and efficiency, while enabling them to voice their concerns and take greater personal responsibility for their own lives.

In short, the internet has the potential to enhance online participation for two reasons: first, because it engages young people on their own terms; second, because most young people have grown up with and regularly interact through social networks, which is why they often see online interaction as a natural means to participate in society. Think about the events that led in 2010 to the uprisings in the Middle East commonly referred to as the Arab Spring. On the one hand, the Arab Spring was facilitated via social media platforms by young people using technology to increase their efficacy and question power. On the other hand, the internet was also used by governments to monitor and censor protesters through digital tracking, thus reinforcing the authoritarian regimes that the uprisings were intended to undermine. This suggests not only that digital technologies offer opportunities and risks in general and more specifically for democratic participation, but also that pupils can only exercise their rights as citizens in the digital age provided they learn how to navigate such risks and opportunities.

Civic participation

Besides enhancing political knowledge and participation, use of digital technologies can enhance children's and young people's opportunities to be civically active and help others within their communities. The internet, in particular, can be a place to learn about socioeconomic issues such as famine and poverty that demand compassionate and caring responses. Using digital technologies not only contributes to children's and young people's ability to appreciate these matters, but also provides them with a tool to do something about them.

The internet has become the easiest and most convenient way for children and young people to reach out to and help others. It has made it possible for them to show a social conscience and connect with people from the same or different communities without leaving their homes. Children and young people are increasingly using the internet to set up campaigns, organise fundraising events, volunteer in their communities and get people together in the interest of supporting good causes. The internet has, in some cases, been the fuel behind a new wave of youth social action – one that has enabled younger users to make a meaningful contribution to the world around issues such as migration, social justice and the environment.

> As found by Demos in November 2013, around 340,000 young British Facebook users had interests related to social action, and around 150,000 tweets were identified as discussing social action. The specific forms of social action that interested users differed by gender: females were more interested in volunteering and males in protest and activism.

Although digital technologies can enhance civic participation, it is important to remember, and to discuss with pupils in and outside the classroom, that there are potential negatives to the moving online of volunteering and social action. One of these is the fact that it is now far easier to click a link and think this may be enough to help others – an issue often referred to as clicktivism. Relatedly, this issue can lead to moral licensing – that is, to children feeling they have done a good deed by signing an online petition without having to do something in the offline world. Another flip side is that too much time online can prevent children from spending valuable face-to-face time with others, especially those who might need more help.

LEARNING EXPECTATIONS AND SCHOOL POLICIES

This section provides an overview of how the digital risks and opportunities that we have explored link to the six objectives of the Futureproof framework, as discussed in part 2. We will outline the learning expectations that pupils might pursue as a result of the framework being introduced to schools, which would require the delivery of targeted lessons in line with learning expectations and the implementation of targeted school policies.

The following tables provide a summary of the learning expectations and related policies. The text that follows discusses the tables and their implications in more detail. It is important to note that there is a learning expectation for each of the framework's six objectives, and each objective, in turn, relates to each of the risks and opportunities presented by digital technologies. It should be emphasised that the learning expectations are not linear, but in many cases build on each other. With this in mind, the tables that follow could be used as a formative tool to monitor how the framework may be implemented.

DIGITAL RISKS: LEARNING EXPECTATIONS

	Abuse	Crime	Privacy	Mistrust	Wellbeing
Cultivate a common digital vision	Pupils want to eradicate different forms of online abuse, from cyberbullying and trolling to revenge porn.	Pupils want to interact online with either no or minimal and manageable risks to their or other people's safety or security (e.g. in relation to grooming, extremism or issues of fraud and scams).	Pupils want to have a positive digital footprint that enhances their life and career, while also wanting to promote a digital environment that is less privacy-invasive and reliant on data tracking.	Pupils want to contribute to a shared sense of digitally mediated trust in others and institutions, while also wanting to promote authenticity and critical thinking in relation to their own exposure to online content and their own digital interactions.	Pupils want to use digital technologies to enhance their and others' wellbeing, as opposed to experiencing negative issues of mental and/ or physical health, from excessive screen time to access to inappropriate content.
Develop a shared digital literacy	Pupils know and understand what online abuse is (e.g. cyberbullying, trolling), why it is wrong and how to deploy digital skills to minimise or prevent their exposure to it (e.g. by blocking or reporting other users).	Pupils know and understand issues of online safety and security risks and how these can be minimised by deploying digital skills (e.g. by reporting groomers to online platforms or by managing their security settings).	Pupils know and understand the risks of sharing information and communicating online, how this might impact their futures, and how to deploy digital skills to minimise the tracking of their data and have a positive impact on their digital footprints (e.g. by managing their privacy settings).	Pupils know and understand why truth and trust are important in the digital age, and how they can deploy critical thinking and digital skills to evaluate and promote the authenticity and reliability of the online content that they are exposed to, as well as the authenticity and reliability of their own digital interactions (e.g. by comparing and contrasting different sources online or by sharing their own selfies without excessively resorting to the use of filters).	Pupils know and understand how digital technologies might adversely affect their and others' wellbeing, and how to deploy digital skills to minimise the impact (e.g. by tracking how much time they spend online or by using filters that prevent them from being exposed to inappropriate content).

	Abuse	Crime	Privacy	Mistrust	Wellbeing
Implement a commonly agreed set of policies	School implements policies to reduce (i.e. to prevent and/or deal with) different forms of online abuse (e.g. cyberbullying, trolling) in and out of school (e.g. by having policies defining when pupils, staff and visitors can use mobile phones on school premises).	School implements policies and other measures to reduce (i.e. to prevent and/or deal with) issues of online safety and security (e.g. grooming, extremism, fraud) affecting their pupils (e.g. by having policies and procedures in place for how to respond to specific online incidents and concerns).	School implements policies to help pupils learn about privacy in the digital age and manage their privacy online (e.g. by having a safer technology use policy that covers managing personal data, email use, sharing videos and photos).	School implements policies to promote a culture of trust and authenticity and reduce pupils' exposure to, and the proliferation of, misinformation (e.g. setting expectations of school's, staff's and pupils' use of social media).	School implements policies and measures to reduce the negative impact of digital technologies on pupils' wellbeing (e.g. by ensuring issues related to wellbeing and digital technology use are covered in the PSHE curriculum).
Co-develop and uphold guidance on netiquette	Pupils follow guidance and communicate with each other online with greater respect, civility and kindness, in ways that minimise their exposure to risks related to online abuse.	Pupils follow guidance and interact online in ways that reduce risks related to online safety and security (e.g. by avoiding interacting with users who ask for sensitive information).	Pupils follow guidelines that help them to develop a clean and positive digital footprint (e.g. by avoiding posting photos of themselves that may be misjudged by potential future employers).	Pupils follow guidance that helps them to interact with online content and others in ways that are underpinned by trust and authenticity (e.g. by privileging reputable sources when accessing information, or by limiting the extent to which they use filters when sharing selfies).	Pupils follow guidance that helps them to look after their and others' wellbeing (e.g. by limiting the time they spend online, or by avoiding content that may not be age-appropriate).

	Abuse	Crime	Privacy	Mistrust	Wellbeing
Cultivate digital virtues	Pupils show resilience and bounce back when exposed to forms of online abuse. Meanwhile, they also show compassion so they do not inflict online abuse on others.	Pupils make independent good judgements and avoid risks related to their online safety and security (e.g. by evaluating the pros and cons of interactions that might seem ordinary on first inspection). Meanwhile, they also show integrity by not subjecting others to risks related to safety or security.	Pupils show good judgement about the privacy implications of what they should and should not post online, and of how much of their data is subjected to data tracking (e.g. by evaluating the pros and cons of the kind of data and user-generated content they share on social media platforms).	Pupils are discerning and can critically evaluate the trustworthiness of online content. They are also honest and do not disseminate misinformation online.	Pupils have self-control and use digital technologies with moderation, and only when these enhance their wellbeing. They are also caring and look out for other users' wellbeing.
Nurture digital wisdom	Pupils independently act with wisdom to minimise their exposure to and reduce online abuse (e.g. by choosing the best course of action after evaluating a situation or moral dilemma linked to cyberbullying).	Pupils independently act with wisdom to minimise their exposure to and reduce risks related to online safety and security (e.g. by choosing the best course of action after evaluating a situation or moral dilemma linked to grooming).	Pupils independently act with wisdom to minimise their exposure to and reduce risks related to privacy (e.g. by choosing the best course of action after evaluating a situation or moral dilemma that may impact on the nature of their digital footprint).	Pupils independently act with wisdom to minimise their exposure to and reduce risks related to trust (e.g. by choosing the best course of action after evaluating a situation or moral dilemma linked to the spread of misinformation).	Pupils independently act with wisdom to minimise their exposure to and reduce risks related to wellbeing (e.g. by choosing the best course of action after evaluating a situation or moral dilemma linked to access to inappropriate content online).

DIGITAL OPPORTUNITIES: LEARNING EXPECTATIONS

	Learning	Connection	Leisure	Employment	Citizenship
Cultivate a common digital vision	Pupils want to use digital technologies to positively enhance their and others' learning (e.g. by using search engines to research different topics or by using online learning platforms to access and exchange knowledge and learning materials).	Pupils want to make positive local and global connections that contribute to individual and societal flourishing (e.g. by communicating with others on social media platforms or public forums, or by joining online communities).	Pupils want to use digital technologies to pursue opportunities for leisure and entertainment (e.g. by accessing, producing or sharing videos about hobbies on platforms like YouTube).	Pupils want to use digital technologies that help them to prepare for future employment (e.g. by accessing internship opportunities or by joining professional networking platforms like LinkedIn).	Pupils want to use digital technologies to engage in forms of online democratic participation and take constructive online community action (e.g. by using the internet to e-vote or to volunteer and support social causes).
Develop a shared digital literacy	Pupils know how to deploy digital skills and knowledge to enhance their and others' learning (e.g. by accessing and downloading learning materials from online learning platforms or by deploying an understanding of what social media platforms afford in terms of sharing knowledge and ideas).	Pupils know how to deploy digital skills and knowledge to make positive local and global connections that contribute to individual and societal flourishing (e.g. by using their digital skills and understanding of the affordances of social media platforms to make new friends).	Pupils know how to deploy digital skills and knowledge to pursue opportunities for leisure and entertainment (e.g. by using their digital skills and understanding of digital affordances to access, produce or share videos about hobbies on platforms like YouTube).	Pupils know how to deploy digital skills and knowledge to use digital technologies in ways that can help them to prepare for future employment (e.g. by using their digital skills and knowledge of digital affordances to upload their CVs online or to use professional platforms for networking).	Pupils know how to deploy digital skills and knowledge to engage in forms of online democratic participation and take constructive online community action (e.g. by using their digital skills and understanding of digital affordances to e-vote, seek government information, or use social media platforms to support social causes).

	Learning	Connection	Leisure	Employment	Citizenship
Implement a commonly agreed set of policies	School implements policies to ensure pupils use digital technologies to enhance their and others' learning (e.g. by having policies on acceptable online teaching and learning practice).	School implements measures to help pupils use digital technologies to make positive local and global connections that contribute to individual and societal flourishing.	School implements policies and other measures to help pupils use digital technologies to pursue opportunities for leisure and entertainment (e.g. by ensuring pupils learn about technology use, wellbeing and leisure in the formal and informal curricula).	School implements policies and other measures to enable pupils to use digital technologies in ways that help them to prepare for future employment (e.g. through an expectation that pupils learn how to use new and emerging technologies for employment).	School implements measures to enable pupils to use digital technologies to engage in forms of online democratic participation and take constructive online community action.
Co-develop and uphold guidance on netiquette	Pupils follow guidance and instruction when using digital technologies for learning (e.g. by respecting rules on how to download learning materials or interact with others on online learning platforms).	Pupils follow guidance and instruction that helps them to use digital technologies to make positive local and global connections that contribute to individual and societal flourishing (e.g. by respecting rules of appropriate behaviour when using social media platforms to make new friends).	Pupils follow guidance and instruction that helps them to use digital technologies to pursue opportunities for leisure and entertainment (e.g. by respecting rules of appropriate behaviour in the context of accessing, producing and sharing videos about hobbies online).	Pupils follow guidance and instruction when using digital technologies in ways that help them to prepare for future employment (e.g. by respecting rules on how to best behave on professional platforms for networking).	Pupils follow guidance and instruction when using digital technologies to engage in forms of online democratic participation and take constructive online community action (e.g. by respecting rules of appropriate behaviour in the context of voicing their civic or political concerns as part of online communities).

	Learning	Connection	Leisure	Employment	Citizenship
Cultivate digital virtues	Pupils deploy virtues when using digital technologies to enhance their and others' learning (e.g. by showing curiosity and intellectual humility when using online learning platforms).	Pupils deploy virtues when using digital technologies to make positive local and global connections that contribute to individual and societal flourishing (e.g. by acting with compassion and honesty when communicating with others on social media platforms).	Pupils deploy virtues when using digital technologies to pursue opportunities for leisure and entertainment (e.g. by showing creativity and open-mindedness when producing and sharing videos about hobbies online).	Pupils deploy virtues when using digital technologies in ways that help them to prepare for future employment (e.g. by showing resilience and adaptability when using professional platforms for networking to improve their chances of employability).	Pupils deploy virtues when using digital technologies to engage in forms of online democratic participation and take constructive online community action (e.g. by showing a commitment to social justice as well as civility and respect when voicing their concerns as part of online communities dealing with social issues).
Nurture digital wisdom	Pupils independently act with wisdom when using digital technologies to enhance their and others' learning (e.g. by choosing the best course of action when evaluating a situation or a moral dilemma linked to their use of online learning platforms).	Pupils independently act with wisdom when using digital technologies to make positive local and global connections that contribute to individual and societal flourishing (e.g. by choosing the best course of action after evaluating a situation or a moral dilemma linked to their use of social media platforms to make friends).	Pupils independently act with wisdom when using digital technologies to pursue opportunities for leisure and entertainment (e.g. by choosing the best course of action after evaluating a situation or moral dilemma linked to their use of platforms like YouTube to access and share videos about hobbies).	Pupils independently act with wisdom when using digital technologies in ways that help them to prepare for future employment (e.g. by choosing the best course of action after evaluating a situation or moral dilemma linked to their use of professional platforms for networking).	Pupils independently act with wisdom when using digital technologies to engage in forms of online democratic participation and take constructive online community action (e.g. by choosing the best course of action after evaluating a situation or moral dilemma linked to their participation in online communities concerned with social issues).

These tables provide an overview of what learning expectations and policies may be adopted by schools and teachers with a view to promoting the six objectives of digital citizenship education proposed earlier in the book. Under the premise that the goal of digital citizenship education should be to promote individual and human flourishing in ways that are mediated by the use of digital technologies, the tables show how the objectives of this form of education may be pursued in order to enable pupils to maximise digital opportunities while minimising online risks.

In a nutshell, the tables spell out how children may be better equipped to navigate digital risks and opportunities – from issues of online abuse and privacy to opportunities for learning and citizenship – by developing and deploying a common vision of the digital world (objective 1), digital literacy skills and knowledge (objective 2), and character virtues and wisdom (objectives 5 and 6), while also following general rules of netiquette in terms of how to behave online (objective 4), and more specific rules and policies set by schools in terms of pupils' engagement with digital technologies (objective 3).

To give an example, in order to act as citizens in the digital age, pupils should be equipped with digital literacy, character virtues and wisdom when navigating, for instance, issues of online abuse as well as the potential of digital technologies in terms of citizenship or employment. Although pupils need digital literacy skills and knowledge to block users or report forms of abuse, they also need resilience and compassion to cope with and avoid inflicting abuse in the first place. Similarly, while they need to gain digital literacy in order to use social media platforms to participate in civic communities online or to look for jobs, these opportunities can only be fully pursued if they also learn how to deploy different virtues, from civility to adaptability and a commitment to social justice. At the same time, not only do pupils need to develop a shared vision of the digital world – one that provides them with the motivation required to act wisely and responsibly – but they should also be provided with rules in terms of how to act responsibly online (for example, in terms of what language they may or not may not use within different online settings) and guidance resulting from the adoption of preventative policies by their own schools.

As such, multiple stakeholders should be involved in the task of delivering a character-based approach to digital citizenship education, as outlined in this book. Alongside the role played by pupils themselves as the receivers of this form of education and active users of digital technologies, schools and teachers have a responsibility to deliver formal digital citizenship education, which would involve the development of adequate lesson plans and curricula, as well as extracurricular activities for pupils and their parents. And while schools need to adopt a set of well-defined policies and measures to support the delivery of digital citizenship education (such as the ones included in our framework), other actors such as civil society organisations and policymakers also have considerable roles to play. It would be fair to expect civil society organisations to help raise public awareness about the importance of promoting digital citizenship, and to help develop lesson plans and resources for educators. For this to happen, organisations need to be actively supported by policymakers through adequate financial means as well as legislation. Meanwhile, policymakers also have a responsibility to promote digital citizenship education more robustly through the school curriculum and in ways that make it possible for a unified framework, such as the one proposed here, to be implemented consistently across the UK.

In short, our framework has implications for multiple actors. But it first requires testing and evaluation, which could be achieved by designing and implementing school interventions that tap into the six objectives of digital citizenship education in ways that apply to digital risks and opportunities, as shown by the tables on the previous pages. Promoting digital citizenship education comprehensively and with a more explicit focus on character virtues should be a priority of education research and practice in the digital age. The Futureproof framework is a first meaningful step in this direction.

PART 4
IMPLEMENTING THE FRAMEWORK

INTRODUCTION

In this final part of the book, we show teachers how to implement the digital citizenship education framework in different types of schools and educational settings. Our aim has been to provide a framework that any school can work with and adapt to their context: the three core components and six objectives of the framework are universal and provide a structure that all schools can use to develop their own bespoke and comprehensive approach to digital citizenship education. However, we understand that all schools are different, serving different types of pupils, in different types of contexts, staffed by different types of teachers. They will also be at different stages in their approach to digital citizenship education: some schools will be well advanced, while others will have never thought proactively or strategically about this form of education. It is therefore up to schools to work out how best to implement the framework to meet their needs.

In this part, we provide advice on how the implementation of the framework and local adaptations might be undertaken. The following topics are discussed:

- Getting school staff and pupils on board.
- Appointing a school champion.
- Teacher education.
- Working in partnership with parents.
- Adapting the framework to meet diverse needs.
- Evaluating impact.
- Sources of further advice and support.

We conclude with a list of organisations that can offer further resources, advice and support on the topics covered in the book.

GETTING SCHOOL STAFF AND PUPILS ON BOARD

Any new whole-school initiative can only be implemented if significant backing and effort is provided by senior leaders; they must believe in the framework and make time to ensure it is implemented successfully. School leaders will have their own approaches to implementing new school-wide initiatives and will know what works in their settings. In this section, we offer one approach to change management that we believe, after local adaptation, provides a series of steps that any school leader can follow.

There are several popular models for change management. One of the most popular is John Kotter's eight-step process for leading change, which was developed by Dr Kotter after watching how different types of organisations implemented change.[117] We like the model because it is practical and aligns well with the implementation of our proposed approach to digital citizenship education in schools. Below, we outline the eight steps and how they might apply in the present circumstances.

1. **Increase urgency**. Teachers, school staff and pupils need to know that digital citizenship education matters. It is necessary to explain its relative importance to other whole-school concerns, such as attainment and behaviour. This will involve sharing stories with teachers (like the case studies in this book) about the offline implications of the risks and opportunities presented by digital technologies. This stage is crucial to helping teachers and pupils understand why digital citizenship deserves urgent attention.

2. **Build the team**. Ultimately, the framework should have an impact on all staff and pupils in a school, but initially leaders need to identify some key staff to drive the change. They need people with expertise (most likely PSHE, citizenship and computing teachers) and people who can communicate messages. Leaders also need 'doers' – people who can make things happen. The first step would be to form a small working group and agree initial tasks and responsibilities.

3. **Define the vision**. Developing a digital vision is the first objective of the framework and is crucial to getting staff and pupils on board. It must have face value and be context-specific – it needs to speak, in some way, to all those involved in the school.

4. **Communicate**. When launching the framework, it is important that schools circulate information about it through whole-staff meetings, assemblies, parent communications, tutor time and lessons. The framework might be communicated in different ways – for example, the school's version of the components and objectives might be printed on posters and placed visibly around the school. Effective communication would link the framework to the challenges and opportunities associated with living in the digital age (narratives can be very persuasive). It is important that leaders are transparent about the changes that will come with implementing the framework and how these will affect teachers' and pupils' lives and work – for example, banning phones on school premises would be seen as a major change for many.

5. **Get things moving**. There are likely to be some pockets of resistance when the framework is launched. These, initially, are most likely to relate to the digital policies and rules promoted by the framework, as these will be the most visible changes and will involve the most immediate action in terms of behaviour expectations. It is important that everyone is on board and the rules are enforced consistently and fairly. A transparent process of collecting and acting on feedback can help to get things moving.

6. **Focus on short-term goals**. Although the cultivation of digital citizenship in pupils is the overall long-term goal of the framework, this should not be the core focus to start with. The initial task

is to develop a digital vision shared by staff and pupils, and a set of digital rules that provide the foundations for developing competencies, virtues and wisdom. These shorter-term goals and achievements should be recognised and celebrated.

7. **Incorporate change**. Once the framework has been launched, the next step is to reinforce why the change matters and what it consists of. Pupils and staff should be rewarded for achievements in implementing the framework – for example, teaching and learning responsibility (TLR) points may be given to those responsible for implementing the objectives of the framework.

8. **Do not give up**. It is likely that there will be successes as well as failures as the framework is developed and launched. The key is not to give up: it will take time for all the objectives to be realised. Schools and educators should learn from failures and be resilient when faced with challenges. Changes do not happen overnight, and the Futureproof framework represents a long-term vision and includes long-term goals.

APPOINTING A SCHOOL CHAMPION

One way to bring visibility to the implementation of the framework, and to help get school staff, pupils and parents on board, is to appoint a digital citizenship education champion. The role of champion might be made more attractive through financial incentives or time away from teaching to focus on implementing the framework. The tasks carried out by the champion will depend on the school and might include:

- Undertaking baseline surveys to see how the school currently meets the framework objectives and where the gaps are.
- Devising a strategy to launch and implement the framework.
- Working with senior leaders to develop/revise communication around the new framework to ensure it is visible.
- Leading the development of the school's vision for digital flourishing (in consultation with staff and pupils).
- Leading on the development and enforcement of digital rules.
- Ensuring digital literacy, character and digital wisdom are taught across the curriculum and whole school.
- Working with parents to ensure they understand the school's approach to digital citizenship education.
- Monitoring new research on digital citizenship education.
- Monitoring Department for Education/Ofsted and other policy changes that relate to digital citizenship education.
- Learning about and contacting charities and other organisations that offer support and advice on digital citizenship education in ways that are linked to digital risks and opportunities.

The school champion does not have to be an expert in all areas of digital citizenship education – in fact, very few people are. But they do need to be passionate about the subject and know how to organise people to make things happen. The role of champion could extend to being in charge of, or providing pastoral support for, all issues that arise relating to pupils' use of digital technologies, such as sexting, cyberbullying and other forms of abuse. However, in order to perform this role, the champion would need some specialist knowledge, expertise and qualifications (in mental health, for example).

TEACHER EDUCATION

Owing to the rapid rate at which digital technologies, the internet and social media platforms advance, it is important that educators try to keep their knowledge of this area current and up-to-date. This is easier said than done, especially given the general lack of guidance or teacher education on the topic. It is perhaps not surprising that many schools report that they struggle to recruit computing teachers, with one headline saying they are 'as rare as unicorns'.[118] This problem is intensifying: in recent years, fewer teachers are being trained in computer science as their specialism. Ideally, schools would recruit teachers who have expertise in computer science and digital technologies, but we believe it is possible to implement most of the Futureproof framework without this deeper and more specialist knowledge. Specialist technological knowledge will be mostly needed for teaching about some digital opportunities, in particular those relating to employment. What all teachers do need to have is an open mindset about digital technologies – they need to be aware of the risks but open to understanding the opportunities. Although there are disputes about whether pupils can be accurately called 'digital natives', we are attracted to thinking that many adults working in schools today may be referred to as 'digital immigrants' (but, of course, many teachers entering the profession today and in the next few years will have been born in the digital age).

The language of migration helps teachers, especially those who have been in the profession for a longer period, to think about the digital world they are living in. Like most immigrants, they have to learn new rules, a new language and adapt to new cultural and social norms. To implement the framework successfully, teachers must move into the digital world voluntarily and with their eyes wide open. It is ultimately up to them if they want to settle there, but at the very least they must explore the digital world and try to learn about it. After all, good teachers are usually good learners; they are often open to change, adaptable and creative.

It is clear that teachers have a different experience to many of their pupils. This differing experience and knowledge mean that, at times, teachers may be learning alongside, and in some cases from, their pupils. In doing so, teachers are able to expand their understanding of the issues, problems and situations faced by pupils online and, more importantly, their understanding of how they can support pupils in the best way possible.

With this in mind, we must consider the upskilling of staff (pastoral and teaching) in the professional development programmes that are offered to teachers. School leaders might find it helpful to address the following questions.

1. How can schools upskill their staff to help pupils deal with the issues they face online?

2. How frequently are staff provided with opportunities for professional development? Are these opportunities episodic or ongoing? Are they placed in a logical sequence?

3. How do schools train staff in the digital risks and opportunities faced by pupils in a local/regional/national context, which go beyond the statutory requirements of Keeping Children Safe in Education (KCSIE)?[119]

4. What issues or problems faced by pupils in their schools can be linked to digital risks and opportunities?

5. More importantly, do school staff know what support or advice to give pupils in the different situations they might face?

WORKING IN PARTNERSHIP WITH PARENTS

Schools cannot and should not be expected to be solely responsible for digital citizenship education. Whereas schools might be held accountable for a pupil's grades in maths, English and other core curriculum subjects, they cannot be held accountable for how pupils behave online. Whether pupils are cruel or kind, honest or dishonest, is often down to how they have been brought up at home. There are several reasons why they might behave differently online to offline, but, ultimately, they will have learned the core character qualities that make them who they are from a very young age at home.

Although parents might rightly be regarded as the primary character educators of their children and ultimately responsible for how their children use digital technologies, teachers have a vital role to play. Through the Futureproof framework, teachers can ensure that pupils develop skills, knowledge, virtues and wisdom that make it more likely they will flourish online. Schools can help to make what is often implicit more explicit. They can help pupils to make sense of the unplanned and informal education that often takes place at home. They can be a safety net for pupils who do not receive any digital citizenship education at home and whose parents are not great role models. They can also help to fill gaps, because many parents struggle to know what to do, for understandable reasons such as fear of digital technologies, a knowledge gap about how these work, and confusion about the risks and opportunities associated with living in the digital age.

Schools and teachers should not think that by implementing the framework they have sole responsibility for digital citizenship education. They have an important role, but not the sole role. Perhaps on this agenda, more so than any other, they should seek to work in partnership with parents. There are several advantages of working in partnership, including:

- Pupils can receive better digital citizenship education – and considering that character and digital wisdom are largely caught, this is important.

- Teachers and parents can ensure they use the same language to discuss the risks and opportunities associated with living in the digital world.

- Parents can get a steer from schools about what rules are appropriate to manage their children's use of digital technologies.

- Teachers can initiate activities, such as keeping reflective journals, that parents can implement at home.

Previous research has found that there is a communication gap between parents and teachers about their roles as character educators.[120] Research by the Jubilee Centre for Character and Virtues found that although parents and teachers said they prioritised character over attainment for young people, there was a misperception about what the other group prioritised, with both groups believing that the other group prioritised attainment.[121] These findings highlight an issue around how these groups are communicating their educational priorities to each other, and we suspect a similar communication gap exists between parents and teachers when it comes to digital citizenship education.

So, what can schools do to help to close the gap with parents? Here are some ideas:

- Invite groups of parents to co-develop the school's vision for digital flourishing (objective 1) and digital policies (objective 3). They can be consulted through surveys about what the vision and policies should consist of and work alongside teachers (and other stakeholders like pupils and governors) to construct these.

- Run sessions where parents and teachers learn together about the risks and opportunities that children and young people are exposed to in the digital age.

- Encourage teachers and parents to work together to address the dilemmas they face when using digital technologies. There are growing discussions among parents that relate, for example, to when children should be given a smartphone or how much is too much screen time. Schools can host sessions to discuss and facilitate activities around these topics, but these sessions should be run in partnership with parents – it should not be about teachers teaching parents.

ADAPTING THE FRAMEWORK TO MEET DIVERSE NEEDS

In this book, we have combined advice for primary and secondary schools. The main reason for this is that we believe our overarching framework is applicable (after making adjustments for context) to both types of school. We also think that if the primary schools that feed secondary schools share the framework, this will ensure greater consistency in the digital citizenship education that pupils experience. However, by combining advice for primary and secondary schools, we are not saying that older and younger pupils will be exposed to the same digital risks and opportunities – these clearly depend on what access pupils have to technologies and at what age. At the same time, although it is traditionally believed that pupils get their first smartphone when they enter secondary school, this is rapidly changing, with many pupils owning a phone when they start primary school.

If a pupil has unrestricted access to a smartphone, they might be exposed to many or all risks and opportunities presented by digital technologies. For now, statistics show that most of these risks and opportunities really come into focus when pupils enter secondary school. This does not mean that primary pupils should not learn about the risks and opportunities; they should be aware of key issues and primed for these. The character qualities that are central to this book (i.e. digital virtues and wisdom) are developed over a lifetime and are constantly in need of refinement, particularly as digital technologies are always changing.

Teachers need to make a judgement about what access their pupils have to these technologies and how the framework should be applied in their context. For example, if they have pupils who bring phones into the primary classroom, and these are deemed to be destructive, they will need firmer and tighter digital policies than a primary school in which not many pupils have phones. As stated above, digital wisdom is developed over time – it is a developmental concept. We would therefore anticipate that older pupils who have more consolidated critical thinking skills learned through experience may be more likely to hone wisdom. This means that the focus on digital wisdom really comes into effect when pupils are in secondary schools. Of course, they will not always do everything right at this age, but they are more likely to have the critical capacities to reflect on what they might do differently next time and to consider the trickier dilemmas they face when using digital technologies.

At this junction, we want to discuss the transition between primary and secondary school, as this is an important stage in a pupil's life. As suggested above, if primary and secondary schools both implement our digital citizenship education framework, there will more likely be a consistency in approach. Pupils, as they transition, will more likely see a link between their two schools' digital vision, language and rules, and also understand the importance of developing digital literacy as well as character virtues and digital wisdom in order to thrive online and offline. In reality, this is unlikely to be the case. With such a vast number of primary schools feeding into secondary schools, a disparity in knowledge, skills and values is somewhat inevitable. Pupils can arrive in Year 7 with considerable differences in their skills, knowledge and understanding of digital wisdom.

It is important, therefore, for secondary school leaders to map out which essential digital skills, knowledge and values need revisiting after the primary phase, so pupils are better equipped to develop digital citizenship and so schools can implement more robust curricula and policies to support pupils. School leaders from primary and secondary schools must share with each other their evidence and experiences about what their pupils study via the PSHE, personal development and computing curricula, and about what they plan to cover in the future.

Joint curriculum planning between primary and secondary schools is advantageous on many levels. An analysis of previous curricula will allow future learning to be sequenced and built upon, enabling the constant revisiting of previously taught concepts through a carefully mapped joint curriculum. The use and understanding of technical vocabulary may also need to be explored upon transition in order to deal with any misconceptions; the difference in language between settings may lead to confusion for teachers and pupils alike. Differences in approaches – such as the use of mobile phones – must also be considered, as the vast majority of primary schools do not permit mobile phones, which may be in stark contrast to secondary schools, depending on the policy. Similarly, having more access to unsupported online activity may be a new concept for some, and this may raise a need for a good understanding of the school's behaviour policies. At the same time, engagement with parents to understand how school settings vary may be important, with resources made available to support parents in understanding the role they play in cultivating digital citizenship.

Below, we describe other circumstances in which elements of the framework may need adjusting in order to support vulnerable pupils, as well as those with limited or no access to digital technologies.

SUPPORTING VULNERABLE PUPILS

For children with special educational needs (SEN), their vulnerability online is potentially increased owing to social naivety and the lack of social cues available to support their understanding or ability to read situations. There may be a need for more direct instructional teaching about digital citizenship, as opposed to exploratory learning.

Lessons in school may need to be differentiated and broken down into smaller, bitesize chunks. Some less confident pupils may struggle to coherently understand factual knowledge, words and concepts, thereby finding it difficult to create their own schema upon which to build their learning. Constant repetition, in addition to visual resources, may provide support and reduce confusion. One example of possible confusion can arise in teaching about friendship. Some pupils struggle with this concept, considering everyone to be their friend and finding it hard to recognise possible associated risks.

For some pupils, it may be necessary to give clear and specific rules – for example, never give personal details such as your name and address to strangers. These rules, however, may need further explaining in order to avoid confusion – older pupils may be confused about whether or how to give details for the delivery of an online order. When introducing virtues such as honesty, potential confusion can arise around when to be honest. Some pupils may need to explore many scenarios in order to gain a better understanding of challenging situations.

Emphasis needs to be placed on how digital risks could be perceived by the child. For instance, some children may take the risk of someone knowing their address as a literal threat, which can impact negatively on their mental wellbeing by increasing levels of anxiety. Use of language should be carefully considered and the decision of whether technical language is used should be reviewed individually in order to mitigate against confusion or misunderstanding. Some more vulnerable pupils may need specific boundaries, with a focus on what can be accessed and when, and where to get support and help. The involvement of adults outside school may be required to ensure continued levels of support.

PUPILS WITHOUT ACCESS TO THE DIGITAL WORLD

While most pupils have some access to the digital world at home, a digital divide still exists. The pandemic made very clear how many pupils were not able to learn online at home as they did not have access to a computer and/or the internet. It is worth noting that a digital divide also exists between schools: some are much more technologically equipped, while others have very basic computing systems and limited access to the internet. Whether the digital divide is at home or in school, pupils who have less exposure to digital technologies will have fewer opportunities to hone their digital skills, knowledge and wisdom. Of course, it is important to note that lessons about the importance of identified character traits can take place without access to technology, as these should be the same online and offline.

It should also be clarified that, while a basic definition of 'digital divide' refers to a lack of access to digital technologies, digital inequalities exist even when users have access to these technologies. This is often down to a lack of digital literacy skills and knowledge, which are essential for using these technologies functionally and critically. It is therefore imperative that schools provide not only opportunities for access to digital technologies, but also a cohesive approach to digital citizenship education that enables pupils to develop the competencies and character virtues they need in the digital age.

Where schools deem pupils to be at greater risk, perhaps owing to lack of parental support in the home or limited access to technologies, they may have to make specific plans to support these pupils. They may need to provide opportunities for pupils to access a variety of digital technologies and dedicated digital citizenship lessons. It may also be helpful to conduct an audit of in-school resources and how often pupils have access to these. This is possibly more pertinent in the primary sector, to ensure pupils have access to a wide range of resources and digital technologies before transitioning to secondary school.

EVALUATING IMPACT

Much of this book is about implementation and practice. It is about providing digital citizenship education. Our aim is to inspire school leaders, staff and teachers to be more planned and intentional about their whole-school approach to cultivating the skills, knowledge and character qualities that will help pupils to flourish in the digital age. For this reason, most of the book describes practical approaches that we hope teachers can pick up, adapt and use in their school contexts. However, this does not mean we advocate an unreflective approach. As noted earlier in this section, we are not providing a fully formed blueprint: schools and educators have to think about how our framework should be adapted to the pupils and contexts they serve. School leaders and teachers should constantly evaluate the influence and impact of the framework and, if necessary, adjust their practice on the basis of what they find out.

Evaluation is a necessary part of all educational practice – it is essential to know what is working and what is not. We would recommend that, once the framework is first implemented, a plan is made for evaluating its impact. The evaluation should involve various measures: some should be more qualitative (e.g. observations and interviews) and some more quantitative (e.g. questionnaires). Some will be more formative in nature and there is also a place for summative assessment when carried out carefully and well. Overall, the purpose of the evaluation should be to refine practice so improvements can be made. At its heart is a process of group reflection that sees teachers, alongside other members of the school community, as the key agents of change.

When planning how to evaluate the impact of the framework as it is implemented over time, we recommend developing a clear and accessible policy that is shared with all staff and based on the priorities of the pupils they serve. The evaluation policy should:

- Have a clear purpose, one that is mainly formative rather than summative in nature and aimed at learning what can be improved and how.
- Involve the whole school community in the evaluation, including governors, teachers, other school staff, pupils and parents.
- Focus primarily on the digital trends, risks and opportunities that pupils, teachers, staff and parents identify.
- Involve some outside 'critical friends', such as a colleague from another school or a stakeholder from the community.
- Utilise a variety of methods and tools to gain evidence.
- Be embedded and integrated into the school's regular practice.

Below we offer examples of how the different objectives of our digital citizenship education framework might be evaluated.

OBJECTIVES 1 AND 2

Pupils' development and construction of a digital vision and digital literacy skills and knowledge can be measured through written testing – more or less formal in nature. If the aim is to see after one year how well pupils understand their schools' digital vision and have developed digital literacy, random classes can be asked to complete a test. If teachers want to evaluate whether and to what extent pupils' knowledge and competencies have grown, they could run a baseline survey when the framework is launched and follow-up tests each year until they think the framework is fully established in the school.

Examples of evaluation questions that could be used in primary schools include:

- At [insert school name] we have a digital vision to keep everyone _____ [safe].
- List two things that could happen if you did not adhere to the school's digital citizenship policy.
- How can you assess if the information you find online is trustworthy?

- What is the meaning of words such as phishing, trolling, etc.?
- How do you keep yourself safe online? What two things can you do?
- What do you think are the most important character traits to display online? (Some examples may be given for younger children – e.g. honesty, compassion, etc.)
- What does honesty mean online? Are there times when you need to be guarded with your honesty?
- Where can you find more information to support you online, should you need it?
- Who can you speak to if you have concerns online?

Examples of evaluation questions that could be used in secondary schools include:

- Name some of the key features of your school's digital vision.
- Why is the Google reverse image search function potentially useful for assessing the trustworthiness of online content?
- What does 'digital wisdom' mean and why is it important?
- How do you see the relationship between digital rules and digital character?
- Could you give an example of a situation online where digital wisdom could be applied?

OBJECTIVES 3 AND 4

The most accurate way to evaluate whether digital rules and netiquette guidelines are being adhered to is through direct measures. For example, schools could directly measure the number of times their digital rules are broken through spot checks or ongoing monitoring. For spot checks, they might ask staff to count and report, for example, the number of phones confiscated from students in one day, or the number of times cyberbullying incidents related to the use of social media were reported. If schools run several spot checks over the year, they should be able to get a sense of the extent to which their rules and netiquette guidelines are being followed. They could also initiate a more planned evaluation of objectives 3 and 4 over the course of a year. This would involve collecting baseline data about issues such as smartphone use, reported cyberbullying and sexting before the framework is launched. They could update this record once a month using a table like this:

Measure	September	October	November
Number of times teachers observe students using phones in the classroom without permission.			
Number of times phones are confiscated on school premises for inappropriate use.			
Number of times pupils attempt to access inappropriate content on the internet on a school device.			

On-the-spot and continuous evaluations can be supported by asking pupils to complete a survey in which they anonymously report how they and their friends feel about, and how much they adhere to, the digital rules and netiquette guidelines adopted by the school. The data collected from this survey will provide an insight into the prevalence of rule-breaking, although it is important to remember that, owing to social desirability and other factors, it is unlikely that all pupils will report what is happening in their digital lives honestly. The resulting data is therefore likely to provide a picture of what is going on, rather than an accurate record.

OBJECTIVES 5 AND 6

Objectives 5 and 6 are the hardest to evaluate, owing to the nature of character and wisdom. However, they are also among the most important, as they are central to the framework. Although it is not possible to accurately gauge the development of digital wisdom or the growth of digital virtues in pupils, there are measures that schools and educators can put in place that will give them an idea of whether and to what extent these are developing.

One way to evaluate objectives 5 and 6 is through proxy measures. Proxy measures are used when there are no available direct measures of a desired outcome. In this case, there is no off-the-shelf, easy-to-implement measure of digital virtues and wisdom and therefore indirect or proxy measures might be sought. These proxy measures need to strongly correlate with desired outcomes. So, for example, if one of the aims is to enhance compassion as a digital virtue, schools might record the rise or fall in instances of cyberbullying. Likewise, for honesty, schools might record instances of plagiarism.

Given that the development of digital wisdom is the ultimate goal of the Futureproof framework, it might be deemed desirable to devote more time to gaining an accurate understanding of whether pupils are developing this quality. Given the complexity of digital wisdom, it would be impossible to achieve an accurate measure, but it is possible to get a picture of how pupils are developing the four components of the quality:

1. **Digital wisdom literacy**: understanding of the nature of different virtues, and the contexts and ways in which they can be deployed when using digital technologies. This component could be measured by presenting pupils with hypothetical scenarios that involve the use of digital technologies and require them to select one or more virtues relevant to those particular scenarios.

2. **Digital wisdom reasoning**: evaluation of and ability to prioritise different virtues when using digital technologies, particularly when experiencing moral dilemmas depending on context. This component could be measured by presenting pupils with hypothetical moral dilemmas that involve the use of digital technologies and require them to choose the best course of action.

3. **Digital wisdom self-reflection**: reflection on and ability to navigate, when using digital technologies, one's own biases and perspectives and those of others, as well as one's own emotions and those of others. This component could be measured by asking pupils to indicate how likely they are to adjust their own emotions, biases and perspectives when using digital technologies in contexts in which they have to navigate the emotions, biases and perspectives of other users.

4. **Digital wisdom motivation**: desire to act on different virtues in line with a vision of the digital world underpinned by principles of

the common good. This component could be measured by asking pupils to indicate what virtues matter the most to their own sense of self, and to what extent their imaginaries of the digital world align with the digital vision promoted by their own schools.

SOURCES OF FURTHER ADVICE AND SUPPORT

There are many organisations in the UK and further afield that can support schools to enhance their provision of digital citizenship education. Many of these organisations offer support and training as well as free and paid-for resources. We recommend that schools and educators look at the organisations listed below and others for inspiration when developing a strategy for implementing the framework in their specific contexts. We have only been able to provide some sample activities in this book and educators can rely on the organisations below to develop additional activities.

Action Fraud, the UK's National Fraud and Cyber Crime Reporting Centre, is the organisation to contact if pupils have been victims of digital risks relating, for instance, to phishing or scamming. www.actionfraud.police.uk

Association for Character Education is the leading membership organisation in the UK for schools interested in character education. The organisation awards four kitemarks and offers training programmes for schools to enhance their provision of character education. www.character-education.org.uk

Association for Citizenship Teaching supports teachers of citizenship education and offers resources, support and training for schools to help them focus on issues related to digital citizenship education, including media literacy and online participation. www.teachingcitizenship.org.uk

Child Exploitation and Online Protection Command (CEOP) is for teachers or pupils who are concerned that they might have been contacted by a groomer. They can report instances online at: www.ceop.police. uk/safety-centre. CEOP's education website, **Thinkuknow**, provides resources for pupils, teachers and parents covering a range of online safety issues. www.thinkuknow.co.uk

Childnet has lots of advice, support and resources to help parents and teachers educate children about safer internet use. www.childnet.com

Common Sense is probably the best-known charitable organisation working on digital citizenship education, with a focus on parents and teachers. The organisation is based in the US but has branches in many countries, including the UK. It offers a website for educators and a digital citizenship curriculum developed in partnership with Project Zero at Harvard Graduate School of Education. The lessons provided by Common Sense, many of which adopt a character-based approach, relate to everyday challenges and digital dilemmas faced by pupils today. www. commonsensemedia.org

Computer Gaming Addicts Anonymous is a fellowship of people who support each other in recovering from problems resulting from excessive game-playing. www.cgaa.info

Education for a Connected World is a framework to equip children and young people for digital life. bit.ly/3KcKmvK

Get Safe Online is a popular source of information about scams and fraud, and provides general information about online safety. www.getsafeonline. org

Guardian NewsWise is an award-winning news literacy programme for seven- to 11-year-olds that includes a focus on issues such as online misinformation and fake news. www.theguardianfoundation.org/programmes/newswise

Internet Matters is a charity that offers a range of resources and advice on how to educate pupils about digital risks including, for example, trolling. www.internetmatters.org/resources/tackling-online-hate-and-trolling

Jubilee Centre for Character and Virtues is one of the largest research centres in the world to specialise in research on character and virtue education theory and practice. The centre undertakes projects that focus specifically on digital character education. www.jubileecentre.ac.uk

National Bullying Helpline is a service for adults and children who are victims of forms of bullying, including cyberbullying. www.nationalbullyinghelpline.co.uk

Neighbourhood Watch provides information and advice about online extremism. www.ourwatch.org.uk/crime-prevention/crime-prevention-toolkits/terrorism/online-extremism

Parents Against Child Exploitation has a lot of information for parents and professionals about grooming. www.paceuk.info

Prevent is part of the government's counter-terrorism strategy. www.gov.uk/government/publications/prevent-duty-guidance

PSHE Association has lessons and activities that help pupils to 'be internet citizens'. These link to many of the digital risks and opportunities listed in this book, such as misinformation. www.pshe-association.org.uk

UK Addiction Treatment Centres is a private addiction firm that provides help and advice to users who experience forms of internet addiction. www.ukat.co.uk/internet-addiction

UK Safer Internet Centre provides advice (including a five-step guide) to support teachers in helping pupils to take care of their online reputations. www.saferinternet.org.uk/blog/online-reputation-taking-care-of-your-digital-footprint-advice-for-young-people

Wise Kids is a charity that supports educators and parents to help children develop the character qualities and wisdom required to use the internet safely and for positive purposes. A core focus of the organisation is digital literacy, helping young people to develop skills and knowledge that are crucial to using the internet and digital technologies creatively, critically, innovatively and safely. www.wisekids.org.uk

REFERENCES

1   UK Council for Internet Safety. (2020) *Education for a Connected World – 2020 edition: a framework to equip children and young people for digital life*, bit.ly/3KcKmvK

2   www.commonsense.org/education/digital-citizenship/curriculum

3   Department for Education. (2019) *Relationships Education, Relationships and Sex Education (RSE) and Health Education: statutory guidance for governing bodies, proprietors, head teachers, principals, senior leadership teams, teachers*, https://assets.publishing.service.gov.uk/government/uploads/system/uploads/attachment_data/file/1019542/Relationships_Education__Relationships_and_Sex_Education__RSE__and_Health_Education.pdf

4   Department for Digital, Culture, Media and Sport. (2021) *Online Media Literacy Strategy*, https://assets.publishing.service.gov.uk/government/uploads/system/uploads/attachment_data/file/1004233/DCMS_Media_Literacy_Report_Roll_Out_Accessible_PDF.pdf

5   www.childnet.com/resources/kia/know-it-all-secondary-toolkits/lower-secondary-toolkit/digital-citizenship
https://wisekids.org.uk/wk/digital-citizenship

6   See www.jubileecentre.ac.uk

7   We searched on 26 June 2021.

8   Campbell, M. & Bauman, S. (2017) *Reducing Cyberbullying in Schools: international evidence-based best practices*, Academic Press

9   Ribble, M. (2015) *Digital Citizenship in Schools: nine elements all students should know*, International Society for Technology in Education

10 See www.iste.org/explore/digital-citizenship/essential-elements-digital-citizenship

11 www.ikeepsafe.org

12 Harrison, T. (2021) *Thrive: how to cultivate character so your children can flourish online*, Little, Brown

13 Foroohar, R. (2020) *Don't Be Evil: the case against Big Tech*, Penguin

14 The open letter was published on 12 March 2019 and can be found on the World Wide Web Foundation website: https://webfoundation.org/2019/03/web-birthday-30

15   Lazer, D., Baum, M., Benkler, Y. et al. (2018) 'The science of fake news', *Science*, 359:6380, 1094-1096

16   Cocking, D. & van den Hoven, J. (2018) *Evil Online*, Wiley Blackwell

17   Bartlett, J. (2015) *The Dark Net*, Windmill Books

18   Vallor, S. (2016) *Technology and the Virtues: a philosophical guide to a future worth wanting*, Oxford University Press

19   We use the term 'affordances', drawing on the work of the psychologist James J. Gibson (1979), to mean 'what the environment offers an individual'. The term is now regularly used in the fields of technology and society.

20   Vallor, S. (2016) *Technology and the Virtues: a philosophical guide to a future worth wanting*, Oxford University Press

21   Malti, T., Gasser, L. & Gutzwiller-Helfenfinger, E. (2010) 'Children's interpretive understanding, moral judgments, and emotion attributions: relations to social behaviour', *British Journal of Developmental Psychology*, 28:2, 275-292

22   Suler, J. (2004) 'The online disinhibition effect', *CyberPsychology & Behavior*, 7:3, 321-326

23   Orben, A. & Przybylski, A. (2019) 'The association between adolescent well-being and digital technology use', *Nature Human Behaviour*, 3:2, 173-182

24   Definition taken from page 15 in Ribble, M. (2015) *Digital Citizenship in Schools: nine elements all students should know*, International Society for Technology in Education

25   See, for example, Emejulu, A. & McGregor, C. (2019) 'Towards a radical digital citizenship in digital education', *Critical Studies in Education*, 60:1, 131-147

26   Tapscott, D. (1997) *Growing Up Digital: the rise of the net generation*, McGraw-Hill

27   Shapiro, J. (2019) *The New Childhood: raising kids to thrive in a digitally connected world*, Yellow Kite

28   Etchells, P. (2019) *Lost in a Good Game: why we play video games and what they can do for us*, Icon Books

29   Prensky, M. (2001) 'Do they really think differently?', *On the Horizon*, 9:6, 1-6

30   See, for example, Livingstone, S., Mascheroni, G., Dreier, M., Chaudron, S. & Lagae, K. (2015) *How Parents of Young Children Manage Digital Devices at Home: the role of income, education and parental style*, EU Kids Online/LSE

31   See, for example, Dahlberg, L. (2010) 'Cyber-libertarianism 2.0: a discourse theory/ critical political economy examination', *Cultural Politics*, 6:3, 331-356

32   Cocking, D. & van den Hoven, J. (2018) *Evil Online*, Wiley Blackwell

33   John, A., Glendenning, A.C., Marchant, A., Montgomery, P., Stewart, A., Wood, S., Lloyd, K. & Hawton, K. (2018) 'Self-harm, suicidal behaviours, and cyberbullying in children and young people: systematic review', *Journal of Medical Internet Research*, 20:4, 1-15

34 See, for example, the report *United Kingdom Chief Medical Officers' Commentary on 'Screen-based activities and children and young people's mental health and psychosocial wellbeing: a systematic map of reviews'* (2019). Available at: https://assets. publishing.service.gov.uk/government/uploads/system/uploads/attachment_data/ file/777026/UK_CMO_commentary_on_screentime_and_social_media_map_ of_reviews.pdf

35 Orben, A. & Przybylski, A. (2019) 'The association between adolescent well-being and digital technology use', *Nature Human Behaviour*, 3:2, 173-182

36 Livingstone, S. (2009) *Children and the Internet*, Polity

37 Prensky, M. (2001) 'Digital natives, digital immigrants', *On the Horizon*, 9:5, 1-6

38 Kristjánsson, K. (2015) *Aristotelian Character Education*, Routledge

39 www.gov.uk/government/consultations/online-harms-white-paper/outcome/ online-harms-white-paper-full-government-response

40 See, for example, Humble-Thaden, M.B. (2011) 'Student reflective perceptions of high school educational cell phone technology usage', *Journal of Technology Studies*, 37:1

41 Selwyn, N. and Aagaard, J. (2021) 'Banning mobile phones from classrooms – an opportunity to advance understandings of technology addiction, distraction and cyberbullying', *British Journal of Educational Technology*, 52:1, 8-19

42 Gao, Q., Yan, Z., Zhao, C., Pan, Y. & Mo, L. (2014) 'To ban or not to ban: differences in mobile phone policies at elementary, middle, and high schools', *Computers in Human Behavior*, 38, 25-3

43 Redmayne, M., Smith, E., Abramson, M.J. (2011) 'Adolescent in-school cellphone habits: a census of rules, survey of their effectiveness, and fertility implications', *Reproductive Toxicology*, 32:3, 354-359

44 Lenhart, A. (2009) *Teens and Sexting: how and why minor teens are sending sexually suggestive nude or nearly nude images via text messaging*, Pew Research Center

45 Gao, Q., Yan, Z., Zhao, C., Pan, Y. & Mo, L. (2014) 'To ban or not to ban: differences in mobile phone policies at elementary, middle, and high schools', *Computers in Human Behavior*, 38, 25-32

46 Vallor, S. (2016) *Technology and the Virtues: a philosophical guide to a future worth wanting*, Oxford University Press

47 Harrison, T. (2016). 'Cultivating cyber-phronesis: a new educational approach to tackle cyberbullying', *Pastoral Care in Education*, 34:4, 232-244

48 Kautz, T., Heckman, J.J., Diris, R., ter Weel, B. & Borghans, L. (2014) *Fostering and Measuring Skills: improving cognitive and non-cognitive skills to promote lifetime success*, OECD

49 Kristjánsson, K. (2013) 'Ten myths about character, virtue and virtue education – plus three well-founded misgivings', *British Journal of Educational Studies*, 61:3, 269-287

50   www.jubileecentre.ac.uk/userfiles/jubileecentre/pdf/character-education/Framework%20for%20Character%20Education.pdf

51   Polizzi, G. (2020) 'Digital literacy and the national curriculum for England: learning from how the experts engage with and evaluate online content', *Computers and Education*, 152
Polizzi, G. (2021) 'Internet users' utopian/dystopian imaginaries of society in the digital age: theorizing critical digital literacy and civic engagement', *New Media & Society*

52   Ribble, M. (2015) *Digital Citizenship in Schools: nine elements all students should know*, International Society for Technology in Education

53   https://hfh.fas.harvard.edu/measuring-flourishing

54   This measure is not psychometrically sound as it is untested. For further information on the psychometric properties of the original measures, see:
Węziak-Białowolska, D., McNeely, E. & VanderWeele, T.J. (2019) 'Flourish Index and Secure Flourish Index – validation in workplace settings', *Cogent Psychology*, 6:1

55   This is a very Aristotelian view of flourishing – he thought it was the ultimate purpose of human life. For a fuller discussion of the nature of human flourishing, see Kristjánsson, K. (2021) *Flourishing as the Aim of Education: a neo-Aristotelian view*, Routledge

56   Polizzi, G. (2020) 'Digital literacy and the national curriculum for England: learning from how the experts engage with and evaluate online content', *Computers & Education*, 152
Polizzi, G. (2021) 'Internet users' utopian/dystopian imaginaries of society in the digital age: theorizing critical digital literacy and civic engagement', *New Media & Society*

57   Quigley, A. (2018) 'Vocabulary knowledge and the "Frayer model"', *The Confident Teacher* (blog), www.theconfidentteacher.com/2018/04/vocabulary-knowledge-and-the-frayer-model

58   Woolcock, N. (2021) 'Phones should be banned from classrooms, mental health coalition says', *The Times*, www.thetimes.co.uk/article/phones-should-be-banned-from-classrooms-mental-health-coalition-says-xhqj7pcgb

59   Woolcock, N. (2021) 'Locking phone pouches help students learn the art of conversation', *The Times*, www.thetimes.co.uk/article/locking-pouches-give-pupils-a-break-from-smartphone-habit-h3k2w2drz

60   www.childnet.com/blog/online-etiquette-or-netiquette-the-dos-and-donts-of-online-communication

61   www.jubileecentre.ac.uk/1844/character-education/teacher-resources/the-character-curriculum

62   www.jubileecentre.ac.uk/userfiles/jubileecentre/pdf/insight-series/GP_TH_IntegratingCyber-WisdomEducationintotheSchoolCurriculumFinal.pdf

63   Department for Education. (2021) *Keeping Children Safe in Education 2021:*

statutory guidance for schools and colleges, https://assets.publishing.service.gov.uk/government/uploads/system/uploads/attachment_data/file/1021914/KCSIE_2021_September_guidance.pdf

64 www.jubileecentre.ac.uk/1844/character-education/teacher-resources/the-character-curriculum

65 Livingstone, S., Mascheroni, G. & Staksrud, E. (2018) 'European research on children's internet use: assessing the past and anticipating the future', *New Media & Society*, 20:3, 1103-1122

66 https://core-evidence.eu/updating-the-4cs-of-online-risk

67 Palladino, B.E., Menesini, E., Nocentini, A., Luik, P., Naruskov, K., Ucanok, Z., Dogan, A., Schultze-Krumbholz, A., Hess, M. & Scheithauer, H. (2017) 'Perceived severity of cyberbullying: differences and similarities across four countries', *Frontiers in Psychology*, 8

68 Andersen, I.V. (2021) 'Hostility online: flaming, trolling, and the public debate', *First Monday*, 26:3, https://firstmonday.org/ojs/index.php/fm/article/view/11547

69 John, A., Glendenning, A.C., Marchant, A., Montgomery, P., Stewart, A., Wood, S., Lloyd, K. & Hawton, K. (2018) 'Self-harm, suicidal behaviours, and cyberbullying in children and young people: systematic review', *Journal of Medical Internet Research*, 20:4, 1-15

70 Ibid.

71 Tokunaga, R.S. (2010) 'Following you home from school: a critical review and synthesis of research on cyberbullying victimization', *Computers in Human Behaviour*, 26:3, 277-287

72 Whittaker, E. & Kowalski, R.M. (2015) 'Cyberbullying via social media', *Journal of School Violence*, 14:1, 11-29

73 Smith, P. (2014) *Understanding School Bullying: its nature and prevention strategies*, SAGE Publications

74 Smith, P.K. & Berkkun, F. (2017) 'How research on cyberbullying has developed'. In Mc Guckin, C. & Corcoran, L. (eds) *Bullying and Cyberbullying: prevalence, psychological impacts and intervention strategies*, Nova Science

75 Madigan, S., Anh. L. & Rash, C.L. (2018) 'Prevalence of multiple forms of sexting behavior among youth: a systematic review and meta-analysis', *JAMA Pediatrics*, 172:4, 327-355

76 Research undertaken by Erika Rackley: www.birmingham.ac.uk/schools/law/research/spotlights/ibsa.aspx

77 www.gov.uk/government/publications/revenge-porn

78 Refuge. (2020) *The Naked Threat: it's time to change the law to protect survivors from image-based abuse*, www.refuge.org.uk/wp-content/uploads/2020/07/The-Naked-Threat-Report.pdf

79   www.gov.uk/government/publications/revenge-porn

80   Centre for Strategy & Evaluation Services. (2019) *Rapid Evidence Assessment: the prevalence and impact of online trolling*, Department for Culture, Media and Sport, https://assets.publishing.service.gov.uk/government/uploads/system/uploads/attachment_data/file/973971/DCMS_REA_Online_trolling__V2.pdf

81   Ibid.

82   www.nspcc.org.uk/what-is-child-abuse/types-of-abuse/grooming/#types

83   HM Government. (2015) *Counter-Extremism Strategy*, https://assets.publishing.service.gov.uk/government/uploads/system/uploads/attachment_data/file/470088/51859_Cm9148_Accessible.pdf

84   Dutton, W.H. & Shepherd, A. (2006) 'Trust in the Internet as an experience technology', *Information, Communication & Society*, 9:4, 433-451

85   See Goffman, E. (1959) *The Presentation of Self in Everyday Life*, Doubleday

86   Gardner, H. & Davis, K. (2013) *The App Generation: how today's youth navigate identity, intimacy, and imagination in a digital world*, Yale University Press

87   BBC News. (2013) '"Selfie" named by Oxford Dictionaries as word of 2013', www.bbc.co.uk/news/uk-24992393

88   McCabe, D.L, Butterfield, K.D. & Treviño, L.K. (2012) *Cheating in College: why students do it and what educators can do about it*, Johns Hopkins University Press

89   See, for example, Liu, M., Wu, L. & Yao, S. (2016) 'Dose-response association of screen time-based sedentary behaviour in children and adolescents and depression: a meta-analysis of observational studies', *British Journal of Sports Medicine*, 50:20, 1252-1258

90   Initial findings from the Millennium Cohort Study Age 14 Sweep (2017-18) can be downloaded here: https://cls.ucl.ac.uk/cls_research/initial-findings-from-the-millennium-cohort-study-age-14-survey

91   The report *United Kingdom Chief Medical Officers' Commentary on 'Screen-based activities and children and young people's mental health and psychosocial wellbeing: a systematic map of reviews'* (2019) can be downloaded here: https://assets.publishing.service.gov.uk/government/uploads/system/uploads/attachment_data/file/777026/UK_CMO_commentary_on_screentime_and_social_media_map_of_reviews.pdf

92   Lay, K. (2021) 'Social media use linked to higher levels of depression', *The Times*, www.thetimes.co.uk/article/social-media-use-linked-higher-levels-depression-7g7gfl2dd#

93   Geddes, L. & Marsh, S. (2021) 'Concerns grow for children's health as screen times soar during Covid crisis', *The Guardian*, www.theguardian.com/world/2021/jan/22/children-health-screen-times-covid-crisis-sleep-eyesight-problems-digital-devices
Auxier, B., Anderson, M., Perrin, A. & Turner, E. (2020) 'Parenting children in the age of screens', Pew Research Center, www.pewresearch.org/internet/2020/07/28/

parenting-children-in-the-age-of-screens

94   A term coined by the social science professor Sherry Turkle in her 2011 book of the same title.

95   Woolcock, N. & Papworth, H. (2021) 'Schools must act over futile TV watershed, says Ofsted head', *The Times*, www.thetimes.co.uk/article/527d2ab0-2619-11ec-9d7f-240ccd0a3a50?

96   Ofcom. (2021) *Video-Sharing Platform Guidance*, www.ofcom.org.uk/__data/assets/pdf_file/0015/226302/vsp-harms-guidance.pdf

97   www.ofcom.org.uk/news-centre/2021/better-protections-from-harmful-online-videos

98   Wright, P.J., Tokunaga, R.S. & Kraus, A. (2016) 'A meta-analysis of pornography consumption and actual acts of sexual aggression in general population studies', *Journal of Communication*, 66:1, 183-205

99   Campbell, D. (2019) 'Depression in girls linked to higher use of social media', *The Guardian*, www.theguardian.com/society/2019/jan/04/depression-in-girls-linked-to-higher-use-of-social-media

100 Lemov, D. (2020) *Teaching in the Online Classroom: surviving and thriving in the new normal*, Jossey-Bass

101 Liu, M., Wu, L. & Yao, S. (2016) 'Dose-response association of screen time-based sedentary behaviour in children and adolescents and depression: a meta-analysis of observational studies', *British Journal of Sports Medicine*, 50:20, 1252-1258
     Neophytou, E., Manwell, L.A. & Eikelboom, R. (2021) 'Effects of excessive screen time on neurodevelopment, learning, memory, mental health, and neurodegeneration: a scoping review', *International Journal of Mental Health and Addiction*, 19, 724-744
     Twenge, J.M., Joiner, T.E., Rogers, M.L. & Martin, G.N. (2018) 'Increases in depressive symptoms, suicide-related outcomes, and suicide rates among U.S. adolescents after 2010 and links to increased new media screen time', *Clinical Psychological Science*, 6:1, 3-17

102 Mitchell, M.E., Lebow, J.R., Uribe, R., Grathouse, H. & Shoger, W. (2011) 'Internet use, happiness, social support and introversion: a more fine grained analysis of person variables and internet activity', *Computers in Human Behavior*, 27:5, 1857-1861

103 Gauntlett, D. (2018) *Making is Connecting: the social power of creativity, from craft and knitting to digital everything* (second edition), Polity

104 Jenkins, H., Shresthova, S., Gamber-Thompson, L., Kligler-Vilenchik, N. & Zimmerman, A.M. (2016) *By Any Media Necessary: the new youth activism*, New York University Press

105 Dezuanni, M. (2018) 'Minecraft and children's digital making: implications for media literacy education', *Learning, Media and Technology*, 43:3, 236-249

106 Etchells, P. (2019) *Lost in a Good Game: why we play video games and what they can do for us*, Icon Books

107 Saleme, P., Dietrich, T., Pang, B. & Parkinson, J. (2021) 'Design of a digital game intervention to promote socio-emotional skills and prosocial behavior in children', *Multimodal Technologies and Interaction*, 5:10, 58

108 Cellan-Jones, R. (2018) 'Digital skills gap opens up in English schools', BBC News, www.bbc.co.uk/news/technology-44518612

109 Russon, M. & Hooker, L. (2021) 'UK "heading towards digital skills shortage disaster"', BBC News, www.bbc.co.uk/news/business-56479304

110 WorldSkills UK, Enginuity and the Learning and Work Institute. (2021) *Disconnected? Exploring the digital skills gap*, https://learningandwork.org.uk/resources/research-and-reports/disconnected-exploring-the-digital-skills-gap

111 McKinsey & Company. (2020) 'Beyond hiring: how companies are reskilling to address talent gaps', www.mckinsey.com/business-functions/organization/our-insights/beyond-hiring-how-companies-are-reskilling-to-address-talent-gaps

112 Meneses, J. & Mominó, J.M. (2010) 'Putting digital literacy in practice: how schools contribute to digital inclusion in the network society', *The Information Society*, 26:3, 197-208

113 *The Times*. (2021) 'Spoon-fed pupils are far from ready for our high-tech future', www.thetimes.co.uk/article/spoon-fed-pupils-are-far-from-ready-for-our-high-tech-future-wf7q6hvf9

114 www.bcs.org

115 Boulianne, S. (2020) 'Twenty years of digital media effects on civic and political participation', *Communication Research*, 47:7, 947-966

116 Trechsel, A., Kucherenko, V. & Silva, F. (2016) *Potential and Challenges of E-voting in the European Union: EUDO Report 2016/11*, http://hdl.handle.net/1814/44926

117 Inspired by www.kotterinc.com/8-step-process-for-leading-change

118 Tes. (2019) 'Are computer science teachers as rare as unicorns?', www.tes.com/news/are-computer-science-teachers-rare-unicorns

119 Department for Education. (2021) *Keeping Children Safe in Education 2021: statutory guidance for schools and colleges*, https://assets.publishing.service.gov.uk/government/uploads/system/uploads/attachment_data/file/1021914/KCSIE_2021_September_guidance.pdf

120 Harrison, T., Dineen, K. & Moller, F. (2018) *Parent-Teacher Partnerships: barriers and enablers to collaborative character education – initial insights*, University of Birmingham

121 Ibid.